LES DAWSON GIVES UP

LES DAWSON
GIVES UP

Giving Up Things
That Are Bad For You

by
Les Dawson

PAPERMAC

First published 1989 by
PAPERMAC
a division of Macmillan Publishers Limited
4 Little Essex Street London WC2R 3LF
and Basingstoke

Associated companies in Auckland, Delhi, Dublin, Gaborone,
Hamburg, Harare, Hong Kong, Johannesburg, Kuala Lumpur,
Lagos, Manzini, Melbourne, Mexico City, Nairobi, New York,
Singapore and Tokyo

ISBN 0-333-49824-0

A CIP catalogue reference for this title is
available from the British Library

Typeset by Wyvern Typesetting Ltd, Bristol
Printed by Richard Clay Ltd, Bungay, Suffolk

Contents

Author's Note

I love that. 'Author's Note' makes me feel quite the academic. In this modest classic, page two will follow page one for the hard of hearing and hopefully being on top of each other, the words should be easy to read.

I would like to thank my family for their help in buggering off whilst I got on with the writing of this book. My thanks to Poo, the lovely woman in my life who read all the pages as I typed them and got the doctor to come out and have a word with me.

My thanks to the lads in the pub, bless you wherever you all lie.

Finally, my grateful thanks to Midshipman Clott who sent me his memoirs of service aboard a Swiss frigate and his experiences as the one chosen to go in the barrel.

Hope you enjoy reading this mammoth work of art. I enjoyed writing it and I feel sure that it will help to guide the reader through the traumas of life today. There are excerpts that will chill the blood of sensitive folk so when you glance through it, sit near a fire.

As they say in East Borneo, 'Shifi naffi tagha bioingo.' I have used that expression many times when pulled up for the breathalyser and it's never let me down.

Les Dawson

A Somewhat Jaundiced Introduction

I live in a society that tells me quite firmly that everything I say and do, eat and drink is bad for me. When I mouth a mother-in-law joke, some outraged citizen from Dulwich (they all seem to complain in Dulwich) will scribble furiously to the BBC that I am a sexist, and should be bundled off to an atoll with a used Gideon.

As a quiz master, I frequently plant a kiss on a nervous contestant . . . especially if she's pretty. That gesture earns the comment, 'He's a dirty old sod!' from viewers who must think a kiss is the Gateway to Hell. If we are indeed fashioned in the image of God, then I'm sure He'd do the same on a celestial *Blankety Blank*.

Frowning dieticians in off-white coats grab me by the throat and inform me of the perils of smoking and drinking; they thunder to me that my eating habits will kill me – I must eat fibre and exist like some sort of albino salamander. I'm rapidly becoming an endangered species because I won't jog or hurl myself about with Jane Fonda.

So what does the future hold for the human race? We'll no longer puff tobacco or drink spirits or have sex in case we finish up being told off by Mary Whitehouse. There is absolutely no doubt about it . . . the day will dawn when we will all die of nothing.

The other lunchtime in a pub, I devoured a plate of chips and sausages and a thin woman in a track suit attempted to horsewhip me.

Frankly I'm fed up with all of you. Just leave me alone with my adored flab, let me die on my terms, reeking of alcohol, wreathed in Woodbine fumes and clutching a snap of a Page Three girl. If I want to give up something, I'll jolly well do it, but I flatly refuse to have some loping idiot from an institute *making* me do it.

This book is intended for those of you who would like to give up something, if only for Lent, without seeming to do it, if you get my drift. Like Oscar Wilde, I believe that the only way to fight temptation is to give way to it ... although in some aspects of moral behaviour I think he went too far; I don't want to get funny looks in South Kensington urinals.

Before the letters from Dulwich start to arrive in buckets, let me ask you a question. What lives longer, a sparrow or a turtle? The answer? A turtle. The sparrow flies about endlessly and never stops whistling; the damn thing is always on the go and eventually it drops dead in a nervous heap. The turtle seldom moves a muscle unless it wants a pee and spends most of its time doing nothing, except living almost for ever (well, until some awful accountant wants turtle soup in Claridges). It is my fervent belief that Sloth is the key to a long and satisfying life. My idea of extreme exertion is reaching across a pale blonde nude to get room service.

I love a drink, in fact I love a lot of drinks ... Don't get me wrong, I'm not a hard drinker, I find it easy. I recall with some bitterness that I was once three minutes late for opening time at a public house and brewery shares slumped. That is the sort of regard I'm held in. I've curbed my smoking habit most effectively, I only smoke now between meals. Last Tuesday I had fifty-three dinners.

What is the point in having a liver if it doesn't have anything to do? Why should I carry it around with me? Cigarettes make

2

me cough, so that keeps my lungs active and paying attention.

I remember when my Uncle Bert passed on; he never smoked or drank and he thought sex was something that educated people put coal into. As he lay in his coffin, my mother said, 'He looks well, doesn't he? That week in Bognor did him good.' For Christ's sake, Mother, he's dead! Incidentally, I'm not apologising for the old 'thought sex was something educated people put coal into' gag. I couldn't think of a decent new one, I was being fitted for an appliance at the time.

So, my friends, here is my offering to enable you to Give Up Things: a veritable treasure trove for the inadequate; a necessary tomb for the average urban failure. Remember the words of Colonel Gower Pickles, just as he attempted to swim the Channel with an anvil strapped to his chest. He said to his mistress, 'Glu . . . glu . . . glug.'

What is life but a theme for quips?

... and Sir Walter Raleigh marched through the assembly towards his beloved monarch, and she smiled tenderly upon her favourite scourge of the high seas.

'What have you brought me this time from the New Worlds, Sir Walter?' the Queen said heartily, with a hint of avarice in her voice.

Raleigh knelt and bowed his head in homage. 'Pray put this between your lips, Your Majesty, and allow me to set fire to the end of it.'

The Court gasped. Had Raleigh gone too far?

Queen Elizabeth did as Sir Walter asked her, and as the end of the thing was ignited, she coughed and spluttered. 'What the hell do you call that, Wally?'

Sir Walter Raleigh replied proudly, 'It's called a potato.'

Why people should find giving up smoking difficult is quite beyond me. Also may I add, why should you want to give up smoking? Oh yes, the Greybeards told you to. I forgot. You want to live for ever and giving up fags will stop you paying VAT for eternity. But have you considered another fact? The longer you live, the longer you will have to fork out vast sums of money to bland men in pin-striped suits for the privilege of haunting this vale of tears in search of a decent mortgage rate.

All right, you want to live to be a hundred and give your relatives a bad back from lifting you up and down off your commode, and cigarettes may very well cut you off in your prime so they have to go. The first thing you must do, and I can't stress this strongly enough, is to stand naked in a draught in order to catch a cold, which should then turn into rheumatic fever and point the way to a very sore throat indeed. If you survive the Last Rites, the sore throat will put you off smoking for a bit and you can throw up every time you chew a Fisherman's Friend.

To some lesser mortals, this initial method of breaking the habit is too arduous, so let us examine another way to beat Madam Nicotine. Light up three cigarettes at once, shove them in your mouth and inhale briskly. With luck this should cause you to lose your voice but alas, there is a problem with this system. Your wife may think you've something to hide by not speaking and she may well go back to her mother ... On the other hand that may not be a problem but a blessing, especially if her mother lives in Tibet.

No, I believe standing naked in a draught to start with is by far the best method, particularly if the woman next door wishes to stop smoking as well ...

Right, you've done the buff state and you haven't touched a cigarette for three whole days and you now feel that you are the master of your own destiny ... But a word of warning, the craving will come back as soon as the throat expands into health. The worst time of all is when friends drop in and light up in front of you. The answer is to get a new set of friends who don't smoke and send the others a poison pen letter wrapped in a lung section.

What really helps at this stage is to be a family man, because the craving is so acute, you'll need people around who you can scream at or club to death. (In the case of some of my relatives, I hired an assassin, but they are frankly unreliable and keep begging to be sent back to Iran ...)

It's a messy time, and sobbing openly doesn't help matters a jot – so lock yourself away, preferably with a bottle of Scotch, and play a Max Bygraves album. If the whisky doesn't send you reeling into a coma, Max Bygraves will.

In the morning, stay in bed and pull all the hairs from your legs until the pain drives the thought of a cigarette from your mind. I know quite a few chaps who came to enjoy this practice so much they started pulling the hairs from their chests and eventually their heads. By the time your legs are denuded, it should be time for bed again and by midnight, after you've bandaged your appendages, sleep should come – helped, I might add, by running at the wall with your head lowered.

It is now a week since the last cigarette, and you feel fine apart from mild concussion and advanced dysentery. Loneliness is something you have to live with, I'm afraid . . . because (a) you are beginning to smell and (b) you are a pain in the arse.

Ten days have elapsed since the last cylinder of Ole Virgini' touched the taste buds, and you don't feel any better for your abstinence. The wife has to hide the kids from you, you might lose your job because you threatened to butcher the office staff, and you are eating everything that no longer has a pulse. The clean-shaven appearance has surrendered to a set of sinister jowls and the bags under your eyes are so big, it looks as if your nose is wearing a saddle. Usually, at this stage of decay your lips swell up alarmingly and take on the form of a set of moist inner tubes. God-fearing folk will tend to avoid you and in rural areas, the elderly will wreathe themselves in garlic.

Please, I implore you, keep away from weighing machines. If there is one in your neighbourhood, vandalise it immediately, or get an adult orphan to do it. Experience shows that you will put on weight, and with the price of clothing today, I strongly advise that you take to wearing bin liners when you visit the pub. It should be a novelty for the lads and it makes it easier to put you to bed when you're pissed.

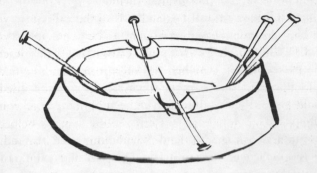

There are those who attest to the virtue of hypnotism as a means of stopping smoking: beware, say I. A friend of mine who was a three pack a day man was given treatment by Dr Hans Schemmingfester, formerly of the Zurich Clinic for the chronically withered. You may recall that the good doctor was the first man to prove beyond a shadow of a doubt that people who ate prunes were never late for work. Schemmingfester was a dressmaker in Berlin before he became a Nazi with an all-dwarf Polish flute orchestra. His gift for hypnosis emerged during the war when he put a cow in labour to sleep. He was awarded the Iron Cross for opening Arab dustbins in the heat of battle and, through a hypnotic trance, he was able to move Rommel's bowels. When the holocaust ended, Schemmingfester, thanks to a homosexual relationship with a British officer, was able to come to these shores and set up as a freelance brain surgeon in Crewe. The chances are that he would have remained in that occupation but for a quirk of fate. A motorist on the M1 swerved across the central barrier and crashed into a charabanc because of the pain his piles were causing him.

Schemmingfester happened to be on hand when the accident occurred, and he removed the motorist's piles. Unfortunately, being a brain surgeon, he brought the man's piles out through his head. He was instantly struck off the medical register and had his licence endorsed. Two years later, he opened his hypnosis clinic in Wolverhampton and married the leader of a strike picket outside a chicken-pox vaccine factory. She created a lot of interest in the press when she caught the disease, because it was the first time in living memory that a picket had been pocked.

But to get back to my friend. Schemmingfester treated him by hypnotic suggestion, using the Pavlov's dogs stimulation method. Every time my friend craved for a fag, Schemmingfester, with his patient in a deep trance, would ring a little bell and howl like a canine. It cured my friend of smoking, that I agree – but every time he heard a bell his eyes would cross and he would spring forward on all fours and make love to a Jack Russell terrier. His wife threatened to divorce him unless he did it in a street where nobody knew him. Frankly, for my few cents' worth, I am against hypnosis as a means of stopping smoking . . . or would you rather be a mule?

There is strong evidence to suggest that acupuncture may alleviate the need for tobacco, but once more, a word of caution. Any solicitor will tell you, for a small fee, that is, of the case of Rivingdale-Dribble *v* The Peking Needle of Health Company in Bayswater. Mr Dribble was pierced with over fifty needles in vital areas. It didn't stop him smoking and every time he drank a glass of water, it shot out of the holes. The holes in his ears whistled loudly in high winds and his face was frequently smacked by an outraged lady of mature years . . . Mark you, he scored once or twice with an ex-nun who had a lot of catching up to do.

Now that you have kicked the habit, let us see just where it has got you. Your weight has increased to such an extent that every time you bend your knees your eyelids fly open. Nothing fits you properly and you've been asked to resign from the Masonic Lodge. Was it worth all the trouble? Okay, the cough's gone and you can taste your food better, but if you've ever been in McDonald's do you really want to taste it?

We exist in an age of fringe lunatics who, if they had their way, would have heavy smokers hunted down and shot by peculiar men in Land Rovers. Pipe smokers would be sent to a big house on a hill for treatment, and cigar smokers would be beaten up by union leaders at Ford's and made to do a week's cabaret in a Northern working men's club.

As for snuff takers . . . death by having the nostrils blocked up with corks.

Why should smoking be so terribly anti-social? Red Indians did it before giving Custer a good hiding, and certainly Dyak headhunters enjoyed a puff or two after a fillet of missionary. Who are these zealots who insist that everything is bad for us? Are they reformed smokers? I hardly think so – they are too busy banging their heads against a wall.

I hope that you have not been plunged into a deep depression by all that has been written, because there is an easy approach to this business of giving up smoking. I have called it simply 'The Dawson Contra-habitual Investigative Directive of Moral Transdigressional Behaviour in Retrospective Corybantics Indigenous to Humanitarian Social Idealism'. Excuse me for a moment, I think I'm going to fart.

Giving Up Smoking the Dawson Way

I know, I know, you've been waiting for this with bated breath and I can't blame you. The thing is, it's so easy to do if you follow my tutorship to the letter. (Don't send any cash at this point.)

Prepare to be staggered. First, you don't give up smoking. What you do is as follows: you stand with your buttocks close to the fire and you trumpet loudly to all and sundry, 'I am giving up smoking.' Your family will rise to their feet with tears streaming down their loving faces and you will be a king. That very night the wife will bestow her favours upon you and your eldest son won't borrow the car.

Then I suggest that you visit a theatrical costumier's in London and purchase a set of whiskers, creep into a gents' convenience and glue them firmly to your chins. You are now ready to enter a tobacconist's shop in a disguise that will fool anyone and purchase several large cartons of your favourite brand. The next items for purchase are a pocket-sized battery-driven fan to be used for clearing the air around your person after a puff or two – and, of course, a large bottle of aftershave and some pellets to cleanse the mouth.

Now comes the tricky part . . . Find some excuse to send the family away for a few days – Bulgaria's quite handy actually, but failing that, Robin Hood's Bay isn't too bad – and then hide packets of cigarettes in various sections of the house. May I suggest taping a packet inside the toilet cistern? One spends many happy moments in the vicinity (unless one has been fool enough to indulge in a vindaloo curry). There has to be a packet in the bedroom of course and don't forget the garden shed. Sew packets into the lining of your dinner jacket and other suits and, frankly, I would pin one or two fags to your underpants.

The stage is set: people believe you have stopped smoking and invitations are rolling in for cocktail parties. You are, sir, a paragon of virtue and an all-round good egg. Imagine the glances of admiration you will bask in during a lunchtime session in the pub. You of all people, known to be a heavy smoker, actually standing with your cronies, pint in hand and refusing a cigarette. Personally, at this juncture I would be tempted to boom in a loud voice, 'No thanks, I've given up the filthy habit, but if *you* must smoke just go ahead.'

After half an hour you will be choking for that stream of smoke down the lungs, so off you trot to the toilets, enter a cubicle, remove the pantaloons, fidget in the elastic of your drawers for one of the cigarettes pinned there, light up with gusto and inhale with unbridled joy. Adjust your attire, blow away the fumes with your minuscule fan in case any suspicious friend has trailed you into the loo, and squirt aftershave about your person.

If you are a very heavy smoker, it is obvious that you will be making lots of trips to the lavatory and this could create a doubt among your compatriots ... All you have to do, if questioned about the frequency of these visits, is to mumble audibly that you have a bladder problem. A really close associate will say that he'd never noticed that complaint before, to which you reply that it flared up again when the X-ray you had taken clearly indicated that the shrapnel had moved lower. Straight away, there is an air of mystery about you. The barmaid will lean closer and play merry hell with your hormones as you whisper diffidently that the War Office have slapped an embargo on your army service, and then turn slightly sideways and mutter something about a DSO. Drop in names like Tito, Korea, Russian defectors and if someone nudges your arm, wince noticeably and say it only aches in wet weather.

The worst part of the deception is over. At home, you merely stretch and tootle off to the nearest cache of cigarettes, puff away and return to the ardent gaze of a misled wife.

Fag ash can be a devil and I venture to suggest that you buy a small vacuum cleaner that can be strapped to your back with the nozzle down the side of your vest. Merely shuffle to an electric plug socket, bung the juice on and suck the ash from your clothing. Obviously the lump up your back where the vacuum cleaner is stored will cause comment, but if you say that your doctor advises you to walk with a stoop so as to prevent future slipped discs, you may get away with it (unless the doctor in question is a big mouth in which case blackmail is the only answer). Frankly, any decent tailor can make provision for the hump and believe me it is well worth the expense. Remember also that the sight of a hump will ensure that somebody gives up his seat to you on the Tube.

There is growing concern about the ban on smoking in public places, and this is a thorny one and no mistake. There wasn't one heavy smoker who didn't feel the chill when this edict was announced, and many habitual draggers were buying up small islands in the Hebrides in the hope of puffing their lives away in peace (the weather being what it is up there, the rain soaked the fags to shreds and gave them all a ginger moustache).

A lapsed draughtsman from Morecambe came up with the answer: a long tin cylinder secured to the inner thigh with a long rubber tube and mouthpiece that could be stowed under the armpit with a rivet. All one has to do before going to, say, a theatre, is to blow reams of cigarette smoke into the cylinder, seal it up, and Old Bob's your uncle. The cylinder can be uncomfortable – especially if you get cramp – but the sheer ecstasy of burying your face in a bag of toffees, which hides the tube as you inhale deeply, is worth the effort. (Do remember to hold your fan under your hat at the same time.)

To all intents and purposes you have stopped smoking, and you haven't lied; you have stopped smoking in front of other people and that is sufficient. So to recap . . . You need things to freshen your mouth, which can be kept in a leather satchel taped to your chest. A vacuum cleaner, a small fan, a receptacle for the smoke, should you be fool enough to go to a pantomime, and a bottle of aftershave which is easily secreted in a truss.

There is one small point which I damn near overlooked and that is nicotine stains on the fingers – always a problem and one not easy to solve. Quite obviously you cannot be seen with a cigarette holder unless you have a friend in the ballet, so the answer is to use oven gloves. Your wife's chums will think you do all the cooking and will look at you tenderly before going home to give hell to their husbands. Oven gloves can look quite trendy and when not in use, they can be hung down the back of your neck.

There is bound to be some comment about your appearance, but in the long run people will get used to it and in the meantime it will serve to keep the in-laws away. Mr C.B. Footbinder wrote to me from Halifax:

Dear Sir,
    It works! It really works. I've got all the equipment you mentioned and I'm smoking more cigarettes than ever. I had rubber sheaths put around my knees to stop the tin cylinder from banging them and the wife dyed my oven gloves to match my cardigan. The vacuum cleaner up my back helped me to get an audition for a remake of 'The Hunchback of Notre Dame' and soon I might be able to give up my job at the Post Office.
    Yours most sincerely,
        C.B. Footbinder
        PS My intimates call me Betty.

Need I say more on this subject? Surely the proof is in the pudding.

You can send money now if you like.

. . . so it came to pass that a hardened drinker found himself in the dock at the Old Bailey on a charge of attempting to shoot his mother-in-law. He pleaded guilty to the offence and said that the attempted shooting was due to the curse of drink. He then thundered to the judge, '*I missed her*, Your Honour, which also demonstrates the curse of drink.'

Single track mind

I approach this subject with a great deal of trepidation, my friends, because I have only been totally sober once and then the dog bit me as I opened the front door. (When she saw me my wife said, 'What a nasty bite, have you put anything on it?'

'No, my sweet potato,' I replied, 'the dog ate it as it was.') Thus we face the first peril of sobriety: without drink, nobody recognises you and you could end up phoning the Samaritans.

Frankly, I suffer from chronic alcoholic constipation . . . I can't pass pubs. Can you imagine a world without boozers? Those dimly lit havens where pints of liquid ambrosia surge down the clack valve until your legs concertina beneath you as the last note of 'Nellie Dean' splutters from your throat. Those sturdy comrades who fold you in half and bung you into a taxi – where would you ever find pals like that if it wasn't for pubs? There is no way whatsoever that throwing up in a Chapel of Rest can equal the sheer robust ecstasy of regurgitating down a barmaid's apron after a darts match.

The Romans drank and they lasted pretty well, and the Ancient Greeks never turned a blind eye to the old noggin, did they? Suddenly, however, society thunders that alcohol isn't good for us any more as we grope towards physical excellence and mental apathy. One never sees those magnificent noses nowadays; wonderful olfactory organs that were plum-coloured sonnets to strong liquor. My grandfather's hooter had so many holes in it, he could whistle 'Dixie' through it. The veins on the bridge stood out in a geometric pattern and after a keg or two of Guinness, it looked rather like the Ipswich rail terminus. He was a wonderful drinker and I seldom saw him standing upright. He went on a day trip to Calais and drank so much wine, they had to pay duty on him at the Customs. He always said he would leave his liver to science but when he died they contested the will. We shall never know how much he supped the night he passed on, but three weeks later you could still smell his breath at the inquest.

His manner of passing is still talked about in various inns. By all accounts he fell into a barrel of rum and it took him six

hours to drown . . . Mind you, he got out of the barrel five times to go to the gents'. I went to visit his grave recently – you can't mistake it, the only thing that grows on it is hops.

It is my firm belief that drink is essential for a long and active life. Alcohol pickles the organs, does it not? Take the case history of Rathbone Mole, the celebrated actor and fish manure specialist. Mole always knew when he'd had enough . . . he used to fall down, and he did it a lot. Rathbone Mole wasn't born in a trunk at a theatre, he was born in a hospital; it was when his father saw him that he put him in a trunk. His mother, the celebrated diva Madame Gerta Bugari, whose performance as a Peruvian nun going bald in a cupboard is still the talk of Hull, had her son educated and brought up at Eton. Many people who met Mole said he looked as if he'd been eaten and brought up. Mole was a tall thin man with protruding ears and he often did an impression of a wing nut. From the moment he entered drama school, his taste for alcohol became a legend. To obtain money for drink he stole anything he could lay his hands on, but his shortsightedness led to his arrest when an eagle-eyed private detective spotted him trying to pick pockets in a nudist camp. A lenient judge put him on probation after Mole promised to give up the demon drink, and the judge was so pleased at his desire to reform that he joined him for a few beers after the trial.

Mole didn't just see pink elephants, he married one, and he shuffled off his mortal coil at the grand old age of eighty-seven. His autopsy proved beyond a shadow of a doubt that throughout his life he had been nothing more than a perambulating distillery. A pathologist (who shall be nameless because of his infatuation with a Bunny Girl) swore on oath that he had to strangle Mole's liver in the laboratory when it tried to bite the end off a thermometer to get at the liquid inside.

So what are we to make of all this? Of course you may blurt out that Rathbone Mole was the exception, and that evidence clearly shows that imbibing alcohol is dangerous to a person's well-being and I will accept that – as well as money if you've got any. But you see Mole isn't alone . . . My Aunt Cissie, a noble lady by any standard, brewed carrot wine by the bucket, and the stuff was lethal. The blessing was, not only did it make you seriously pissed but you could see better. Now Aunt Cissie lived to the ripe old age of ninety-five and died beautifully preserved with two of her own teeth left. Do you see what I'm getting at? Surely if you drink enough then it's bound to sort of mummify you, isn't it?

My research into the effects of alcohol on the human condition took me into many public houses and little else, but I learned a lot: how to cadge drinks off an estate agent and how to allow the body to go limp prior to its being hurled into the street by a landlord. The public house is the nub of British society and if these traditional places for sots are ever closed, then husbands will have to stay at home and fight with the wife. If it wasn't for the public house, no Chancellor of the Exchequer could ever raise enough duty to pay for increased social benefits for Punjabi stone-cutters. Is it not the vices that help support the virtues in a democratic state?

Let us take an hypothetical situation . . . Alcohol has been banned from these shores and all traffic wardens are Methodists. Something else will then have to be taxed in order to pay for the motorways to be torn up, but what? Obvious, isn't it? Sex. Suddenly, the healthy normal activity between men and women will assume the same sort of sinister overtones that alcohol was tainted with. Couples will be wired up and monitored between the sheets and excess passion will result in an increased Copulation Tax as well as profound cramp. There will be a Black Market in condoms plus VAT and woe betide those who indulge in a knee trembler without a provisional licence.

If there's one thing guaranteed to spur you to give up drinking even faster than a new Budget, it's a visit to your local quack. I say quack because in my experience most doctors are . . . quacks. Take our neighbourhood pill dispenser – he's so old-fashioned he still lances a boil on horseback, and his idea of pain relief is to make you bite on a bullet. I heard last week that he might have to retire . . . he's running out of leeches.

The doctor examines you very thoroughly, and his face assumes a grim expression. As you pull your knickers back on, he speaks in a monotone that oozes foreboding . . . 'Quite apparent that you have been abusing your body, old chap . . . too many late nights, hey? Blood pressure is so high, if it wasn't for your skin you'd be a fountain . . . Ha ha ha.' In a single examination you are found to have brain damage, kidney failure, liver pollution, high blood pressure, a heart murmur, a partial erection for which you are grateful, a sagging prostate, and piles. When he's finished his scathing diatribe, you genuinely wonder how you've lived so long. The verdict is clear. You must give up alcohol.

Three weeks have elapsed since you last had a drink and isn't it getting easy? The trouble is, when you go out for an evening, it's you who does the driving and you've supped so many orange juices you are beginning to look like a sullen tangerine – all the lads keep taking the pith. Some idiot suggests that you start drinking non-alcoholic lager which dries the mouth into a Tunisian wadi and makes you pee a lot more. Parties are an ordeal and frankly you are so boring you could send a glass eye to sleep. You don't feel any better and, inevitably, you snap and eagerly quaff a brimming tumbler, then another, and you're back to square one – the only difference being, of course, that you will drink more heavily than before and look for a new doctor, preferably one who drinks as well.

Worry no more, help is at hand within these pages, help that has been drawn from years of experience. Personally I cannot exist without a hangover – it gives me a feeling of martyrdom when the wife throws my bacon sandwiches to the dog and moves into the spare room. As we discussed in the How to Give Up Smoking campaign, it is quite essential for you to become shifty in your habits, and to enjoy lying through your back teeth. Listed below for your perusal are some methods that may be of service in your battle to quit the booze.

The Albert Cattermouse Guide to Sobriety

Albert Cattermouse is a pseudonym for a retired jockey who now works for the Gas Board's sports department and a Morris-dancing team in Kendal. His career as a jockey was not, I hasten to add, one to be remembered. In one race his horse was so slow he kept a diary of the trip. He turned to heavy drinking after he rode a horse that was twenty to one and came in eventually at a quarter to three. The disgrace unhinged him and the horse became a few pints of glue.

For years Cattermouse drifted in an alcoholic fog and his family and friends denied all knowledge of him. His familiar ragged figure could often be seen rummaging in garbage dumps, and when asked why he always had a bottle of gin in his hand, he replied, 'Well, I have to take it out of my mouth some time.' At one stage of his abasement, he used to pick up cigar butts in the street, but he gave that up because he was making some terrible mistakes in the snow.

Then fate took a hand in the shape of Maude Beadlebaum, a Jewish widow of independent means and a bad leg. She fell in love with Cattermouse while she was performing in a charity variety show in a Limehouse soup kitchen. Maude had a fine soprano voice that had once filled the Albert Hall – the audience had made room for it. She refused to marry Cattermouse until he stopped drinking and, so infatuated was he, he went straight to the A A (but actually joined the R A C). His idea of Alcoholics Anonymous was to drink in places where nobody knew him. Finally, he hit on a solution which has recently been published by Peake & Capp (price £5.50 with nothing back on the empties).

In essence it is a simple method of staying sober . . . Drying Out. Briefly, the theory is that heat draws out the alcohol from the system; and so Maude, bless her bagels, purchased a large industrial spin-dryer and put Cattermouse in it. The old lad would spend hours going round and round inside the dryer as Maude blew kisses to him through the glass porthole. When she let him out, Albert would be so dizzy he couldn't even hold a glass, let alone drink from it.

It took only six months to cure Cattermouse. Every time Albert crept to the cocktail cabinet, Maude would hoist him over her shoulder and shove him in the spin-dryer. There were some small side-effects: Albert developed a taste for Bold 3 and his underpants shrank. But now the mere mention of a spin-dryer is sufficient to turn him into a trembling teetotaller.

Drying Out the Cattermouse Way

Fourteen revolutions for people who drink less than a quart of spirits a day. Keep on medium heat until face purples. For heavier drinkers, it is advisable to spin faster for the first wash-out of the system on high heat. Keep patient's feet turned inwards and elbows knotted together. Allow the face to press against the glass porthole as it can be as good as television. Never put clothes in with the patient in case it makes the colours run. When released, the patient will keep on rolling for the remainder of the night, so make sure that all the doors are firmly secured in case he or she cartwheels in front of a bus.

This method is not advisable for fat drunks – all too often, their backsides stick out and spoil the effect of the new kitchen units. Industrial spin-dryers are quite expensive, so on no account have them serviced with someone still inside. Screws and washers can be mislaid this way and give some patients acute bowel problems, especially if they are long screws. Mark you, there are those among us who might find the length very agreeable.

This, in a nutshell, is the Albert Cattermouse Method – one which many people will not find to their taste, but believe me it does work. And for dwarfs who want to get fit for pantomime, it's a positive boon.

Tolerance and understanding are prerequisites when dealing with those who get rat-arsed when they go out. (Forgive me, I implore you, for using that vulgarity, but sometimes a shock announcement of that sort can bring attention to this dire problem.) As a case in point, some years ago one of my small group of dedicated barflies imbibed not wisely, but too well of the grape . . . We did not castigate him or eject him from the car. Instead we let him drive because he was too drunk to sing. That, my dear reader, is compassion. (Naturally I do not advocate drinking and driving; if you must drink and drive don't use a car.)

Giving Up Drinking by Hypnosis

This method is used quite often by pygmies who brew their own beer. As they are on the small side, the beer goes to their heads much quicker, if you see what I mean. The danger of heavy drinking with these little chaps is that they frequently make a balls-up with their blowpipes; the darts fly madly about and cause chaos at whist drives.

'Matti pooli bogy humpoo' means 'Oh Christ, he's pissed again.'

It's at times like this that the tribal witch-doctor summons the alcoholic before him, makes him sit on a heap of water buffalo manure, and then slowly waves a dried banana in front of his eyes. Once he has the patient's will, the good doctor chants – and I'll write it in English because my pygmy isn't too good at the moment – 'All things makee very drunk . . . water, 7-Up, cocoa, Bovril.' The witch-doctor snaps his fingers because his bones are very brittle, and the alcoholic comes out of his trance and weaves away to his hut for a large one on the rocks. Meanwhile, having been alerted by the witch-doctor's secretary, the pygmy's wife hands him a jug of swamp water. Because of the hypnosis, he downs the stuff and believes it's a pint of Old and Mild.

The main trouble with this method is that our pygmy is now hooked on swamp water and his wife's left him. But there is merit in hypnosis. In Britain a doctor I've mentioned before, the celebrated Dr Hans Schemmingfester, has had enormous success with it and is having it away with a pygmy. Swamp water is not suggested over here of course – the similarity between it and London beer is too great and could provoke a lawsuit.

Schemmingfester tells the patient in the trance that every time he drinks alcohol a frog grows in his stomach. Now on the surface that sounds ridiculous, but I have seen the results for myself and they are quite staggering. A certain Mr P. from Bournemouth, a devoted alcoholic all his life, underwent this treatment purely in an attempt to discredit Dr Schemming-fester and sell the story to the *Daily Mirror* for a lot of money.

He failed ... miserably, I might add. Immediately after the session with Schemmingfester, he sprinted to the nearest pub and gulped down three large Scotches, two pints of bitter and a martini. Within minutes, he was groaning and begging the landlord to get the frogs out of his stomach. Fellow drinkers watched in horror as Mr P. hopped towards the lavatory. The landlord made a frantic phone call and an ambulance rushed to the scene ... Alas, it was too late for Mr P. He'd croaked.

So you see, there is danger in the hypnotic method, and to be honest I feel it is too complicated a treatment for the average soak. Remember, a frog in the stomach is no better than a toad in the hole.

Of course there are variations in the method. Schemmingfester once told a man under hypnosis that strong drink can harm an unborn child. The man got the wrong end of the stick and thought he was having a baby; he stopped drinking altogether and took up knitting. When he had labour pains, his brother asked if he could be a godmother. Apparently they still don't speak and the hypnotised man rubs himself every night to get rid of stretch marks.

Frankly, and I mean this most sincerely, the only way to stop people saying that you are addicted to alcohol is to employ the following tactics. I can't claim full credit for this scheme, but at the risk of sounding a smart-arse I can vouchsafe that I added a little something to it which gives the method credence. It was actually my brother-in-law who thought up this idea, and if ever a man needed a drink it was him.

My wife would wail at the sight of her brother's legs sticking through pub doors, but as I timidly pointed out, he needed some relief and an escape from a most dreadful hag. That awesome gorgon he had wedded drove him to drink – and for that he was truly grateful – but in the sober moments he experienced occasionally, she opened the gates of hell to him. She never stopped talking for one minute. Her mouth was open so often in winter, they had to lag her tonsils. In fact my brother-in-law has only one decent photograph of her – and that must have been taken with a high-speed camera because it's the only one with her mouth shut.

His intake of alcohol increased with every wedding anniversary, until it reached the stage where he could blow on a birthday cake and light the candles. Then he hit on an idea of how to fool his doctor and his wife. One Monday night, he drank and drank in excess of anything he'd drunk before and when he fell off his bar stool he missed the floor. Because of that binge, he spent a week in a cottage hospital, and for once he could say with all honesty, 'I've not had a drink for a week.' Do you see the logic of it?

My contribution to this scheme was based on pure mechanics. I had a bottle of vodka hung beneath the kitchen sink and hidden behind a sheet of plywood. A tube ran from the bottle to the base of the tap and I drilled a hole into the stem of the pipe that led to the top of the sink and the tap's handle. A simple electric pump placed in an unused teapot was connected to a very small contact switch, situated under the handle of the tap at the rear. When one turned on the tap, water gushed forth automatically, but if one covertly groped behind the tap and pressed the contact switch, the water flow ceased and out shot the vodka through the tap. So there we have what might be called The Contra Flow Method.

Every Monday night, my relation by marriage gets plastered, is taken away to the hospital, spends a week without booze, comes home and says very grandly, 'I've finished with drink . . . all I need is water.' He then takes a large tumbler, operates the mechanism, and downs a vodka. He can now afford to give the hospital a miss for seven days if he wishes, because the food there isn't good and he gets the odd bedsore. His wife crows loudly, 'He only drinks water,' and he occasionally gets his leg over. It's a great method without a doubt . . . He doesn't go to the pub, he stands at the tap all day and although he looks pissed, nobody suspects that he is.

For more information, do send a large cheque and I'll remit a receipt from my villa in Corfu. Failing that I'll settle for a tin of salmon.

... and it came to pass that a thirty-stone man was given some tablets by his doctor in order for him to shed some weight. The instructions on the bottle were quite clear: 'One tablet twice a day.' Unfortunately, the fat man read the instructions wrongly and took three tablets twice daily. Within four weeks he had lost three stone, and after nine weeks he'd lost so much weight that his skin was trailing behind him and his wife had to pull it all up above his head and secure it in a bow.

One day as he was going out, a neighbour studied him and said, 'You're looking a lot better, but that's a nasty gash on your chin.'

The man replied, 'That's not a gash, it's my arse'ole.'

How to Avoid Fatty Foods

We are all aware that the things we enjoy are no good for us, at least that is what the dreary Establishment types keep telling us. What I don't understand is that for centuries kids have sucked toffees and gorged themselves on cream buns, and still gone on to live long lives; years ago people ate fatty foods and a lot of them are still around today. So what are we to make of it all?

This modern society baffles me completely when it comes to food. Chips, sausages, red meat, fried bacon will thicken my arteries until I finally expire clutching a slice of gammon in a disco. When I was a lad, eggs, milk and butter were prized for building a sturdy body, and doctors solemnly advocated these foodstuffs. Now I'm told that they're bad for me, that they could shorten my lifespan, and I won't see my grandchildren get divorced.

I firmly believe that half the trouble is with fashion designers who run out of cloth and then employ thin people to model what's left before the bailiffs move in. The world is skinny mad. If your shoulder bones don't protrude, then you are obese and destined for the knacker's yard. The fashion designers plot with corrupt dieticians and lo and behold, we're all walking around like something out of a Lowry painting. I adore a big underdone steak with hot bulging chips escorting it on the platter; I relish the dribbles of fat oozing between my teeth; as far as I am concerned, if that is going to polish me off, then it's a tasty executioner. Sod the fibre diet, I flatly refuse to spend most of my life on the lavatory. Of course the vegetarians have me by the throat – the pious ones who proclaim that it is wrong to kill for meat. But are they aware that every time they pluck a vegetable from the earth, it screams? It's a proven fact that all living matter possesses an energy field and the death of a carrot is just as dramatic as the pole-axing of a bullock.

We humans really are the giddy limit; we mourn the death of a friend or a loved one, yet we think nothing of stepping on an ant. When you stop to realise that the average healthy ant can lift ten times its own weight, then you know you have just killed a magnificent example of an animated mechanism. At the loss of someone dear, we wail to God and ask why this has happened. Surely if all living creatures have a purpose then God must be a very dispassionate deity who sees Man as no more important than an insect in the greater scheme of things. People think that because we have achieved technical marvels and artistic masterpieces, we are above all else. Bullshit, say I.

How dare pet owners have their cats doctored. Who gives them the right to do it? The poor devils get things thrown at them as they cry at night on a garden wall. Wouldn't you cry if your testes had been scissored off? What can be more tragic for a rampant tom than to see a gorgeous she-cat waving him over to her side of the dustbin and know that all he can do is talk about his operation?

Here I go waffling on again, so let's get back to this diet business before I wax even more cynical, and with an act like mine you'd be cynical as well. The first thing a medical chap will say to you when you go to see him is, 'Lose weight.' It doesn't matter a jot if you are only six stone wringing wet, he'll still tell you to lose weight. That cry is the axis of medical knowledge today, and so off you trot with a heavy heart and throw out the contents of the chest freezer.

Next, you go in for one of those diets that are eulogised on television and in the popular press by ladies with dipstick figures and see-through collar-bones. A calorie-controlled diet sheet will float into your vestibule and on it will be a list of things you *can* eat, in order to slough off the poundage. Are you ready for this?

Salads invariably form the basic ingredients of a diet. Lettuce and more bloody lettuce, tomatoes, cottage cheese and celery are sluiced down with grapefruit juice. Sugar is a bigger enemy than the Third Reich and so you use 'sweeteners' that were probably the by-product of chemical warfare. For breakfast it's bran flakes or prune juice, and an hour on the loo. Within a week, you're wearing National Health blinkers to stop you gazing into shop windows that sell pies and aromatic cooked meats. The thought of more chicken without the skin can send you lurching for a tranquilliser. Every day you step on the

31

bathroom scales – which can never be accurate because of the uneven floorboards – and you shake your head in disbelief when your weight seems the same as before the alps of lettuce you've consumed. The grapefruit at breakfast is costing a lot in toilet rolls and it won't be long before the used tissue blocks up the drains.

The sheer monotony is enough to send you reeling for a biscuit. Then, in deep remorse at your transgression, you find yourself at Weight Watchers, confessing the sin to a church hall crammed with fierce red ladies in crêpe hats. A friend of mine, who was vastly overweight and happy, decided to diet after some urchin shouted out to him, 'Hello fatty.' Personally, I would have bundled the kid off on a freighter bound for the Azores after kicking his diminutive rump with an Army and Navy Stores climbing boot, but my friend took the jeer to heart and his fate was sealed.

Through the grapevine in the pubs and chip shops, I heard that he'd submitted to the Cambridge Diet, the F-Plan Diet and a Scandinavian Banana Diet. When I saw him, I was deeply distressed. He'd obviously gone too far with the bananas because his forehead had broadened out, his nostrils were six inches wide and he walked on his knuckles. He never goes out nowadays. The last time he did, he was picked up in a zoological van and put in a compound. He only got released when someone came to delouse him and found that his backside wasn't as he'd expected.

The following case history of the effects of a prolonged diet is yet another indictment. George was a small man, in fact he wore mudflaps on his underpants. He weighed in at twelve stone and had the appetite of an Indian Army mule. He was a trifle breathless and wobbly on his feet, but a grand lad, at least until his doctor told him his urine was rather peculiar and it was time he shed weight. Six months later he re-emerged into daylight from the limbo of the calorie underworld, and I couldn't believe my old eyes. George was so thin that every time he stuck his tongue out he looked like a zip. He had to part his hair in the middle so he wouldn't overbalance. The good Lord only knows what he'd gone through, but now our once merry little butterball was so emaciated that whenever he drank tomato-juice he looked like a spirit level. Not only had he lost his blubber, he'd lost his sense of humour with it; his suits hung like theatre curtains and he sobbed at the slightest thing. One sad day in March he had a chocolate finger offered him and when he reached out for it, his wife cried, 'No, George,' and hit him with a brass fender. He never had a chocolate finger again because the fender killed him. George's funeral was attended by so many slimmers, it looked as if the graveside was encircled by pea-sticks. Of course with George being so thin, it wasn't worth going to the expense of a coffin, so the undertaker laid him out in a snooker cue case. His widow did three years for manslaughter, then married a pawnbroker with a goitre.

Obviously the tragedy of George is a singular one in the frenzied realm of the slimmer, but it is a point to ponder if you feel you must join the inch war. Meanwhile, for those who yearn for a sojourn on a health farm, allow me to list a few notable spas.

Flab Ranch

Situated six miles from the seaside resort of Miresand-on-the-Crouch, a lovely old town, with tranquil walks from the mine fields to the war graves past the barbed wire warehouse.

During the months of July and August, a Dutch clairvoyant gives lectures on amputations at the end of the ruined jetty. Tea dances are held once every six months in the renovated remand centre, managed by a most charming couple who breed piranha fish in large quantities and are still pro-Franco.

Flab Ranch is a converted convent, which during the fifteenth century was sacked by a group of Flemish smallpox victims. It lies at the foot of a range of hills where, legend has it, many members of the Iceni tribe were buried alive by Roman troops. The ranch has forty bedrooms, most of which overlook Potter's Swamp; the others have panoramic views of a brick kiln and a rupture appliance factory.

Flab Ranch has an indoor swimming pool, and the temperature is the same all the year round (just above freezing point). Wolfgang Schmitt, the supervisor, is a firm advocate of cold water to tone up muscle tissue, and apart from the usual batch of seasonal cardiac arrests, the results are quite good. The gymnasium is fitted with a fibreglass replica of the rack, and there is a rather astonishing treadmill.

It is a strict régime at Flab Ranch. Anybody attempting to have cakes or vanilla slices smuggled in is immediately bludgeoned with a baseball bat and then forced to do fifty press-ups over a bed of hot coals.

In the past there have been various attempts to break out, but the packs of dogs that prowl the grounds do tend to put people off. This may seem a trifle severe, but as Herr Schmitt pointed out to a private detective, 'Vot is der sense in coming 'ere, if dey don't do as dey are told?' There is no news of the private detective and his mother is getting worried.

The diet is carefully adhered to: breakfast is prune juice and half a carrot; lunch consists of a sprig of watercress soaked inside a lemon, with a spoonful of dried herbs; dinner is simply two marrowfat peas on a bed of lettuce and two-thirds of a bean shoot.

The terms for a week at Flab Ranch are reasonable enough: £300 plus VAT with free use of oxygen equipment.

To get there, turn left at Great Yarmouth, follow any sign out of the suburbs and phone the AA.

The Aphrodite Health Clinic

Situated outside Wolverhampton in what used to be a Tudor brothel, the clinic is run by a lapsed Jesuit missionary and the woman he's living with. There are twenty-seven bedrooms with wooden cots and a urinal urn.

Every day a mass jog to Stafford is organised and you are back before breakfast; with hot mud immersion for fat people who've gone lame on the jog. Daily beatings on the naked rump with birch twigs is an added extra to tighten the skin and improve blood circulation. In the past, this method has been severely questioned on account of the number of limp young men who seem to like it.

There is no gymnasium here; exercise is encouraged by a male nurse on horseback with a lance.

For the first week nobody is allowed to eat anything at all, and in cases where the client has a less than iron will, the lips are stapled together. During the second week, a sip of hot water is permitted and a raw chop is given to any lady who feels she's pregnant. Frankly, unless one has served with the SAS or as a cook in the Spanish Foreign Legion, the diet can create problems. I'm sorry to relate that neighbourhood pets have gone missing on many an occasion, and a certain plump Mr Prendergast, who booked in for a fortnight last August, hasn't been seen for some time. The authorities were a trifle concerned at the discovery of his waistcoat, his dentures and a strong smell of chutney.

There is a lot to be said for the activities at the Aphrodite Health Clinic. However, there is also strong evidence to suggest that not as many people come out as go in. A tremendous weight loss is assured, but the mental state of people who have got out sometimes leaves a lot to be desired. Miss Agatha Allsop still looks at her friends and thinks they are chicken pies. She had to be forcibly restrained from shoving her cousin into a microwave oven not so long ago, and her immediate neighbour had to be sedated after Agatha tried to put a pastry crust on her head. On the other hand, there are people who swear by the methods used at the clinic – so it is up to the individual, is it not?

The Aphrodite Health Clinic is rather on the expensive side but if you possess the constitution of an oversexed ox, then you'll find it much to your liking. A week at the Aphrodite will cost you £430 with a small deposit for the birch twigs, as well as tipping the man with the lance to ensure no rectal penetration during the chase.

There are several smaller health farms that offer quite adequate amenities, and I mention two of them before going any further.

Mrs Mulberry's Rustic Fatty Farm

Despite its somewhat juvenile title, the farm is excellently run by Mrs Mulberry, who used to perform on the music hall stage as part of a variety act called The Masked Gurkhas and Winnie. It was, by all accounts, an amusing act in which Winnie (Mrs Mulberry) slid across the stage on a shovel full of braised tripe and played a euphonium as the three Gurkhas set fire to their trousers. She retired when she married Fosdyke Mulberry, who manufactured cork freckles for clowns. Although most petite at the time of her marriage, Mrs Mulberry put on a lot of weight when she lost her husband. He didn't die . . . she just lost him.

She was determined to shed the poundage she had acquired, and did so quite remarkably by having a steam-roller driven across her stomach. Naturally, under the circumstances, this is the method she now advocates to clients. The farm is nothing more than a disused fighter bomber hangar in the village of Nutall Wallop in the county of Avon. One simply books in and undresses before being stretched out horizontally on the concrete floor. With a given signal from a jeep, Mrs Mulberry indicates to a team of steam-roller operatives to commence the first run.

On average, no more than three flattenings are required before a client feels a major difference. However, there have been casualties and Mrs Mulberry does have her share of critics. A certain doctor (Hans Schemmingfester, whom I think I've mentioned before) has said that a lot of people who have undergone this type of treatment find that the only way they can sleep is by draping themselves over a clothes-line. One gentleman who booked in for a week's course at the Fatty Farm had to be rushed to an infirmary after he'd had four runs across his tummy but he's doing quite well in wards 4, 7 and 8.

The cost is £200 for a fortnight and extra for petrol and oil, plus nightly Shropshire laments played on the euphonium by Mrs Mulberry once people stop curling up at the edges.

The Loserlotawate Clinic

Opened in 1983 by an illiterate, this health spa is most unusual in as much as you can eat anything your heart desires, with one slight snag – you are not allowed to swallow it. The method is so easy, it is surprising that nobody has stumbled on it before.

The system is based on the old Roman vomitorium. As any odd scholar will tell you, the Romans used to eat diced dormice and legs of anything that moved, then throw up in a marble vomitorium and start again. Ovid the poet writes of the joy of throwing up with friends to the sound of a lute: 'Nil desperandum sickum' especially if it was windy.

The régime is as follows: egg, bacon and sausage for breakfast; time allowed for chewing; two minutes to savour the taste. Then at the strident noise of a whistle, you spit it all out into a galvanised dish and bury it in the garden. For lunch, steak and chips and peas, followed by apple pie and clotted cream. Thirty seconds is allowed for a chew then out the mess must come into a bucket of straw. Anyone who defaults by trying to swallow the food is made to wear a fright wig and floral knickers and be an idiot for a week. Corporal punishment is sometimes used but at the discretion of the karate-proficient Swiss porters. Running on the spot is encouraged and if you go there make sure you have a big mouth.

Loserlotawate is built on top of a pickle works, designed by Maurice of Turin. Apart from the smell, it's a pleasant enough building and won an architectural prize at the Embassy Rooms, Chiswick. There's an interesting feature in the dining hall – a sixteen by twenty foot painting, 'The Death of Lysander', in early Dulux.

The cost is relatively cheap – £70 per week and a doggy bag at the end of the stay. Directions are straightforward: go left as

if heading west towards South Halifax. Turn round at exit 9 and double back east on the north road left . . . Right?

That's enough free publicity for health farms. Now, we must get down to the nitty-gritty (and not before time, I hear you sigh): this question of losing weight. As we have observed earlier, losing weight entails giving up all the things that make life enjoyable: hot mouth-watering pies with lagoons of thick aromatic gravy; golden crumpets dripping with warm butter; stoutly cut chipped potatoes and fried eggs . . . oh, and let's not forget scalding mugs of sweet tea swishing down sausage or bacon butties. But you have joined the ranks of the Calorie Counters and those naughty treats we've mentioned are a thing of the past, old buddy. You are now obsessed with charts and sheets that angrily point out the perils of carbohydrates and fats and the need for a balanced protein diet. You will have to live with the knowledge of the molecular structure of vitamins, and if you dare munch a chocolate finger, you will be taken out and spanked.

Eat more fish, some will tell you. 'Fish is good for you,' they bray cockily. Have you ever seen what a mackerel eats? With all the pollution in the oceans, I wouldn't give a brass nickel for any fish to complete its life-cycle. My grandmother used to crow at me, 'Fish gives you brains.' If fish are that well equipped intellectually, why do they still get caught? I've yet to see a salmon play chess or a turbot sing something from *Tosca*. Frankly, I was told that there is so much crap thrown into the sea, even atheists can walk on water.

The trouble with a lot of this slimming business, apart from the profit motive, is the subconscious desire to live for ever – to be a Peter Pan. Nobody relishes growing old naturally nowadays. Middle-aged, menopausal males brush their thinning hair forward, wear gold medallions around their necks and swallow vitamin E capsules to enhance their sex drive. And their female counterparts dredge off every ounce of rounded flesh in order to struggle into clinging jeans and yesterday's youth. The silly thing is that Cary Grant and Clark Gable looked better when they were older, and surely no one denies that Liz Taylor has worn pretty well without a silicone implant (although 'tis said that old Liz has had her face lifted so often, she talks through her navel).

Anyway, is it worth all that physical torment just to please a doctor and buy things off the peg?

The Dawson Approach to Psychological Dieting

Strange title? Well, sit comfortably for a spell and let's examine it, shall we? It is my firm conviction (and indeed my father has had many convictions, several at the Old Bailey) that the mind dictates not only what we are, but how others see us.

How to Avoid Fatty Foods

We use such a small part of our brains that one wonders just what we could achieve if the whole area of our topknots was in full operation. At present we seem to be embroiled in so many social trivialities that our true purpose in life has been lost.

I believe that a little deception will not only fool your family and friends, but by using the method laid out below, you will feel thinner without giving up one damn thing . . . Interested?

A year ago, under family pressure due to my ballooning girth, I reluctantly paid a visit to our family quack. (I refuse to say 'doctor' until one of them writes out a prescription I can read – I once had a prescription given me for some antibiotics and I got into a Wembley Cup Final with it.) I admit that I was in pretty poor shape on this particular visit; three days before I had stumbled across a case of fine Scotch, and kept on and on stumbling . . . The only exercise I had undergone for months was shifting the gear stick in my Ford – a car so old it was insured against fire, theft and Viking raids. Late suppers of take-away curries, cigarettes at the ready and the drinks cabinet had turned me into potential mortuary fodder, so it was decided that I should go for a check-up.

As soon as I'd stripped, the clucks of disapproval commenced. The doctor prodded, plundered and pillaged my shivering nakedness, and tutted furiously. He put his digits on and into the oddest places and the fires of embarrassment were stoked higher with every prod. Of course, after the examination of blood pressure and so forth, my condition was critical and I began to wonder if I'd even make it back home. I listened to the learned devotee of Hippocrates with considerable alarm. The theme? '. . . you must lose at least three stone in weight.'

Well, I tried, I really did. No drink, no sugar, no salt, no red meat, spuds or fried foods. At the end of the first week, I muttered, 'Sod it,' to nobody in particular, and made out a will.

If the end was near, I thought, let's make merry, and then I hit upon the idea of psychology . . . or lies if you prefer. I invested a sum of money with a tailor asking him to make three suits for me, each one larger than the previous one. I informed him that I would be using them for a television show and that seemed to put an end to his curiosity, though not the length of his bill.

The first suit fitted my ample contours, and I wore it for a few days, one of which included a return to the quack. He shook his head, tutted and went rather puce as he ordered me back again for another visit within a month. On that next visit I wore the second suit, which was too big for me. The sleeves hid my hands, the shoulders sagged and I needed braces to hold the trousers up near my waist. My medical mentor took one look at me and hopped about delightedly.

'Well done, old chap,' he raved. 'You look better already,' he trumpeted. Dancing around like a mischief-maker, he took my blood pressure and declared it 'much improved'.

See what I'm getting at? He took me at face value. In fact, I felt a lot thinner. When I walked into his surgery in the third suit, which buried me, the sight of it, aided by the extra-large bowler hat down over my ears, removed the breath from his body.

'Good Lord,' he panted. 'Don't overdo it, I beg you.'

This time he declared my blood pressure to be normal and then grasped me around the knees and made me promise to build myself up. At home my wife made me tuck into hot pies and thick gravy and in the pub the lads implored me to drink draught Guinness. Now when I wear the first suit, everybody tells me how well I look, and the strange thing is . . . I do.

DON'T

. . . and it was said that when asked what had happened to his first wife, the old man said gravely, 'She died through eating poisoned mushrooms.'

He remarried three years later and when his second wife died, and caring friends asked him what she'd passed away with, he replied, 'She died through eating poisoned mushrooms.'

Two years later, the old chap met a lady and they married, and on the honeymoon somebody said to him, 'Where's the bride?'

The old man shook his head sorrowfully and muttered, 'She's upstairs in the bridal suite . . . Poor lass is dead.'

Everybody was deeply shocked, and one of his relatives said, 'Don't tell me she's dead from eating poisoned mushrooms?'

The old man replied, 'No, there's an axe through her head.'

The relative paled. 'How the hell did that happen?' he asked.

The old man lit up his pipe and said, 'She wouldn't eat the bloody mushrooms.'

I hardly know how to approach this very emotive subject without appearing to be either a male chauvinist pig or a misogynist; I am not, in any shape or form, a critic of the fair sex. I love women and would love to indulge more in the pleasures of the flesh, but there is a price to pay.

Let's be objective, shall we? Women live longer than men. Why? In my view, it is because of their one great talent . . . making bullets then forcing men to fire them.

To put it bluntly – and I will – women sit on their power. They possess something men want. From the day we squirm out of the womb, we spend the rest of our lives trying to get back in it. You never hear the expression 'Woman born of Woman', do you? So where the blazes do they come from?

It's my theory, based on years of married life, that women are alien beings from some sort of asteroid belt past Uranus. I think they drifted around the galaxy looking for spare parts. Well, they came down here and pinched a rib, didn't they?

No man has ever understood a woman because we don't speak the same language. They in turn never came to grips with our atmosphere on earth, which explains why they have so many headaches and back trouble.

Adam was doing fine, thank you very much, until this naked creature with the wobbly chest and cute bum emerged from the

forest and munched an apple. Adam was awe-struck at this thing before him and wondered why, when she pouted at him, the front of his fig leaf rose into the air. At first he thought something had died down below and rigor mortis had set in, until she reached out and grabbed the pole that was rooted to his groin. Within a minute or so, the pole had sneezed and was now a limp twig. From that awful moment on, Adam was hooked by this alluring stranger with the roving hands and she started to whine for a new fig leaf from the Dior range in return for the exercises on his appendage.

History belongs to women. It is they who dress the stage for the drama of life. Lady Godiva rode bare-arsed down the main road and into the pages of history, but there's never a mention of her husband, Lord Leofric. What about him? Poor old bod must have sat night after night wondering where his missis was and if she had her knickers on in front of the servants . . .

Imagine yourself as a long-suffering husband, sitting near the fire watching your wife undress as she prepares to go out:

Her: 'Won't be long, chuck, just off for a canter down the A5.'

You: 'You've been naked three times this week, can't you stay in just for one night?'

Her: 'Things to do. Mother's coming out with me to the bridge club tonight – I'm going round to help her get her corsets off.'

You: 'You're not taking Mother with you naked, are you? People will think she needs ironing.'

Absurd, isn't it? Yet Godiva's name is still very much alive today. Henry VIII's wives get more attention from historians than he does. Anne Boleyn was a pain in the neck, but not for long, yet her name is associated with the Bloody Tower and old Hal hasn't even got a urinal in the West End he can lay claim to. Women are wondrous but they are the pretenders to greatness, not men. They can survive plagues and thirst, pain and suffering and still keep an appointment at a hairdressing salon. They can give birth to a ten-pound whopper and within five minutes the lipstick's out and they're holding court. They can give a man hell and goad him into making a big decision simply for the sake of peace, and that is called 'guidance'.

They outlive us, outfox us, and outwit us. Men can scorn and best them in a physical trial of strength, but after fifteen minutes in a hot bed she's still at it and he's ready for a coma.

*

From the moment we men start to toddle about, it is Mum who takes charge of us. Oh yes, Dad comes and bounces the Cow and Gate pap out of us, but it is always Mum who's the boss.

It is she who teaches us to walk and talk and then when we do, tells us to sit down and shut up.

As a teenager the average male is merely a mass of spots and an erection. At school we lads drop pencils in order to peep up the lady teacher's skirt; because of women we play with ourselves and feel dirty and perverted. A girl can wear skimpy clothing and flaunt her charms, but if a boy dares to lunge out for her, he's branded a sex fiend and loses his job at the Co-op.

On the other hand, how my mother ever managed to bring the family up I'll never know. Poverty was a constant lodger and Daddy was superstitious . . . he wouldn't work if there was a Friday in the week.

I asked him once if he had ever been offered a job at the Labour Exchange. He said, 'Only once, son – apart from that they've shown me nothing but kindness.'

Feeding her children was a tremendous problem for my mother; she solved it by throwing a bowl of soup into a fan. Food was difficult to obtain. The first time I saw a butcher's shop, I thought there had been an accident. The doctor warned Mum that if she didn't force something down me, my mouth would heal up.

All the clothes we wore were cast-offs and hand-me-downs – I started work at fifteen in a bib, a romper suit and a bowler hat. My sister got married in a truss, spats and a pith helmet.

I always felt sorry for the rentman; he used to come round the neighbourhood, play a violin and busk for his money. You could always tell when he was knocking on the front door – blood used to come through the letter-box.

Yet despite it all, Mum managed and that is the marvellous side of women. It is obvious that we cannot do without them, but how do we avoid the pettiness that sends us to an early grave?

For advice on this problem I turned to Dr Hans Schemmingfester, whose views deserve a wider audience.

In his speech to members of the Home Rule for Bradford Campaign, Schemmingfester laboured the point to several hecklers from an ordnance dépôt that it's not the size that attracts the flies, it's the gyppo round the rim. This stunned the assembly, as well it might. Not since Descartes has a slice of philosophy made such an impact, and remember it was a warm Thursday afternoon in July. In essence, what Schemmingfester was driving at was plainly this: if we can't live without women, we have to live with them – on the male's terms. But how?

Women love mystery and that's a fact. If a man is open with a lady it tends to weaken his stand on any subject, so mystery is important as the first prerequisite for survival. To achieve this, one must begin by deliberately going against her every demand. If she says, for instance, 'No, you can't go to the pub,' you must pull yourself up to your full height and say in ringing tones, so that the neighbours can hear, 'I HAVE TO GO . . .' Stay out late and try to get a drink after time. When you go home, ignore the thrown vase, don't speak, go straight to bed and sob into the pillow.

The following morning she won't speak so that's all right. Just sigh deeply and walk out.

When she asks you to put up shelving, shake your head and say no. Run out and spend the day in the bookie's. Creep back to the house, climb in through the bedroom window, hide in the closet until she enters the room, gets into bed and starts to snore, and then go and put the shelves up.

The next morning when she says what a good job you've made of the shelf construction, bite your lip, accept her kiss on the check, then walk firmly away. By now the wife is in torment and there's no way in the world that she'll go back to her mother until she's found out what you are on about ... Mystery is afoot.

The wife will suspect many things: that you're having an affair, you've gone barmy or that you are a latent gay. Acting on her suspicion, she will obviously get in touch with a private eye, so now you have to lay plans.

Follow your wife until she leads you to the private sleuth she has chosen, then show him photographs of her mother in the bath which will instantly put him on your side – if only from a deep sense of sympathy. That, plus a large sum of soiled currency, will convince him to report your behaviour as you have outlined it to him. If he's a dedicated fan of Mike Hammer, you might have to rid him of his scruples by stealing a body from the city morgue and planting it under his desk before you re-enter the office dressed as an Interpol agent from Istanbul.

The rest is fairly mundane ... Acting on your orders, after a week or so the detective will call at your home and report the following:

Private Eye: 'Madam, I don't know where to begin regarding your husband's activities.'
Wife: 'What has the bastard been up to, and who's the
   floosie he's got in tow?'
Private Eye: 'Yes, there is a woman involved, madam, but
   not a lady of the night ... the lady in question is a
   nun.'

Wife: 'He went through a phase with Brownies once, the dirty sod.'

Private Eye: 'It's nothing like that, madam. He has been helping the nun to collect money for a new convent. Frankly, madam, your husband is a saint.'

At this point, the theatrical agency you contacted to find an out-of-work actress comes up trumps, in the shape of an elderly female thespian clothed as a nun who arrives at the front door just as the sleuth has stunned the wife with his revelations. She prostrates herself before the wife and begs her to allow the nun to see you. The wife stammers that you are at the office. (You're not of course, you are hiding behind a clump of dwarf gladioli.) The nun tells the wife that you are known in the poor areas of the town as 'The White Knight' for your work among the derelicts – that will shake the wife to her very foundations, as she thought you drank with derelicts. Before the actress gets too involved with her rôle and rambles into something from *Wuthering Heights*, she must leave and let the private eye carry on.

He informs the wife of the undercover work you have done for the Vice Squad, by going into public houses and gaining the confidence of known drug peddlers and porn kings and then organising raids to smash the racketeers. If there have been occasions when you have been pissed, the private eye says, it was all in the line of duty, and your efforts have earned you the nickname of 'The Shadow' with the police.

By this time the wife should be in a hell of a state and running back and forth from the loo with excitement. Imagine her feelings . . . her very own husband, a hero, a Man of Mystery.

In one fell swoop, you have totally destroyed her image of the man she married and she is now putty in your hands. When you creep from behind the gladioli later that night, I'll wager she's done her make-up and hair and dinner is on the table waiting for you.

You: 'Hello darling, nice to be home.'

Wife: 'Sit down, my beloved. I bought you a nice piece of undercut. Like a glass of sherry first?'

You: 'Well thank you, dear. I say, you're taking my shoes off and putting my slippers on, how nice.'

Wife: 'I know how hard you work, darling.' (She winks heavily.) 'When you've had your dinner, I suppose you'll be going to the pub?'

You: 'No, love, I think I'll stay in tonight by the fire.'

Wife (arms around you): 'No darling, you must go out . . . my shining Knight . . . my adorable Shadow.'

You (looking at her with narrowed eyes): 'What are you driving at?'

Wife (tenderly): 'Nothing at all, darling, nothing at all . . . I'll be here waiting for you . . . ready for you.'

A quick change and off you saunter to the pub, safe in the knowledge that you have permission to go from a radiant woman. When you totter home she will be in bed waiting for your embrace and you'll enjoy the best leg-over you've ever had.

From that night on, stress will be a thing of the past. She'll do anything for you, and providing you don't get too fanciful, like wearing a cape and a mask and trying to fly from the gable end, life should be pretty good.

Just to be on the safe side, occasionally scan the headlines of the newspaper and mutter, 'What is the world coming to, nobody's free to walk the streets any more.'

The wife will smile and say something like, 'I don't think we've anything to worry about in this town.' She should then get up and fetch your hat and run you to the pub.

So there we have it, in a nutshell: the way to live with the opposite sex without one's nerves jangling like banjo wires. A certain gentleman wrote to me from Hastings, and his letter says it all:

Dear Mr Dawson,

For twenty-two years my life was a living hell. My wife used to beat me on a regular basis and hid my teeth if I tried to go out. I went bald at the age of thirty through nerves and she made me wear a hat all the time, even in the shower. She kept me on the F-Plan Diet until I became so thin I actually slid through my string vest.

I contemplated suicide but after hearing you on a radio programme, talking about Dr Hans Schemmingfester's thoughts on living with women, I decided to try the idea myself.

I hired an actor to play a Russian Army General who told the wife that I was a double agent and a black belt at kung fu. He told her I had killed three terrorists with my bare hands and that I was known in the Ukraine as 'The English Stud'.

It worked like a dream; we now have six kids and I get my tea brought to me in bed.

Thank you so much and I hope you received my cheque.

Yours for all time,

S.M.

How to Give Up Visiting the In-laws

Love is a strange thing and who can understand the emotion? To some people, romance starts with a serenade played on a Neapolitan balcony, to others it's a drift of perfume on a Georgian staircase, and to some, it's the touching of hands in a scented bower. When I first met the wife, I felt a tingle run up my leg – she'd scratched me with her bike clips.

I met my love at a charity dance in Oldham – 'The Friends of the Krays Hotpot Buffet and Dance'. I saw her across the crowded room and nobody had asked her to dance. I'm not saying she was a wallflower but she was standing in the corner in a bucket of bone meal.

That night I took her home in my car. It wasn't a new one, but it had only had one previous owner – Lord Kitchener. The tyres on it were so bald I had to backcomb the treads, and every time I knocked down a pedestrian he got forty lashes as he fell. I had a radio in the car, I remember, but I never used it. I always found it difficult to drive with earphones on and the accumulator on my knee.

I felt the stirrings of lust in my loins as we drove along the lonely road, and my passion increased when she turned to me and said breathlessly, 'Can you drive with one hand?'

I nodded dumbly as my manhood rose.

'Well wipe your nose,' she said, 'it's running.'

Outside her house, I grasped her fiercely and panted, 'Darling, I could live in your eyes.'

She replied acidly, 'You'd be at home there, I've a sty in one of them.'

I was in love . . . terribly, terribly in love. Oh I know that my wife-to-be was no raving beauty . . . Her hair had been dyed so often she had Technicolor dandruff, and her eyebrows were so bushy, it looked as if she was hiding behind shredded wheat. But she did have one remarkable feature – her right eye was very interesting. Well it must have been, her left one kept looking at it.

Despite her bow-legs, I loved her and she was quite bow-legged – in fact she used to iron her knickers on a boomerang. Apparently, when she was a child, her mother used to hang her behind the door for good luck.

Our romance ran the obvious course and we had a quiet wedding (there was a silencer on her father's shotgun). As we stood at the altar, the vicar looked at her, then looked at me and whispered, 'Is this *Candid Camera*?' Outside the tiny chapel, well-wishers threw rice at us, which was kind of them . . . but I wish they'd taken it out of the tins first.

Our honeymoon was spent in Sardinia. We'd only been there two days when a dwarf sprang from behind a tree and snarled at me, 'Stick 'em up! This isn't a banana in your back.' I said, 'Well in that case you'd better stand on a chair . . . you're not in my back.' Oh I know it's legal but sod it, it's not compulsory.

The midget took everything – luggage, clothes, the lot – and left us naked on a mountain pass. My bride shrilled, 'I managed to save the camera and the passports by hiding them in my mouth.' I said, 'It's a pity your mother wasn't with us, then we could have saved the suitcases.' (Quite frankly, I had to clean that remark up.)

So there I was, a married man with all the attendant problems. As the old axiom says, 'You can choose your friends but not your relatives.' How true that old saw is. I cannot think of a more stress-provoking thing than a proposed visit to the in-laws.

Weeks before the trek, you will brood and look for any loophole to avoid the visit. Your work will suffer because of the dire thought of facing that unholy coven. You will eat out of fear, and drink deeply to escape the reality of the event to come. Your blood pressure will go up and down like a yo-yo, and colic will hit the tripes at the mere thought of meeting them again. Already, my friend, your lifespan is in peril . . .

The dreadful day dawns. You didn't sleep very well the night before – you kept having a nightmare in which you were a loose piece of machinery and the mother-in-law was chasing you with a spanner shouting, 'Come here while I tighten your nuts.' You stayed awake half the night, bathed in perspiration, and your wife slept like a baby, with her big toe in her mouth.

In the morning, you feel washed out and ill but there is no sympathy from the better half; she's actually looking forward to seeing that Medusa and her brimstone family . . .

As if sensing your desperate state, the kids are a bloody nuisance, and you keep hiding behind a wall with your hip flask. The car isn't running very well and it stalls at a T-junction. Irate motorists scream abuse at you which harmonises with what you are receiving from inside the car. You lurch off in a wreath of exhaust fumes and a policeman takes his notebook out.

The kids need to pee, the wife wants a cup of tea and you've smoked thirty cigarettes by the time you brake to a halt outside the in-laws' domicile.

The stress shows on you even more as the door opens and your wife's sister, whose expression could make a lemon pull a face, greets you morosely. You walk down the dark forbidding hallway and there, in the lounge, the Family are all assembled:

the father-in-law, looking like a length of coffin bait; the brothers-in-law, Alf and Harry, what a pair of bright farts they are, you could find more life in a tramp's vest; and their wives – Hortense, she's the one who let you in, and the other gorgon, Agnes, who lives constantly in the past and smells rather strong. Some assorted kids are slumped on the carpet, and sitting on the chair near the window is the mother-in-law ... John Wayne in tights.

As usual, you are handed a small glass of unspeakable sherry and on the table is the ritual boiled ham and tongue. The conversation is based on death, near death and acute family illness. And then the past crops up and away we go, slagging off some aunt or other who had it away with a Greek soldier during the Blitz. You are dog tired and the last joke you told died bitterly. The mother-in-law glares at you and watches how many slices of tongue you have put on your plate. One of brother-in-law Alf's youngsters has thrown up on your shoe. Life is now at its lowest ebb and there is no escape from the pregnant boredom. Not one of them is really interested in how you are faring in the big world, and family jealousy is hovering everywhere.

1st Brother-in-law: 'See you've got the same car ... looking rough, what?'

You: 'It's running well at present; no sense in changing it.'

Mother-in-law: 'Alf's doing *so* well these days. At least one of my daughters is all right, thank God.'

Agnes: 'My Alfred bought me a new microwave oven.'

Mother-in-law: 'You've got a good husband there, our Agnes, you never see Alf in pubs.' (She's looking at you all the time she speaks.)

Hortense: 'My Harry's getting promoted soon, aren't you, dear?'

2nd Brother-in-law: 'Well it's on the cards when old Thompson dies.'

Mother-in-law: 'You deserve it, Harry, you've been in that office for twenty-three years . . . Loyalty, that's what I call it, not like some I could mention; can't hold a job down.'

You: 'I have no desire to work in the same job for twenty-three bloody years . . .'

Mother-in-law (sniffing): 'That's why our Gertrude [the wife] will never have the nice things the other two have got.'

You (hotly): 'Just what does that mean, for Christ's sake? Our house is our home . . . not a ruddy showpiece.'

1st Brother-in-law: 'Don't swear in front of Mummy.'

You (half crazed): 'Mummy? For God's sake, man, be your age, and she isn't your bloody mother anyway.'

2nd Brother-in-law: 'Hortense and I have pride in what we've got.'

You (close to cardiac arrest): 'Proud of what you've got? Living in that piss-hole you call a house? All the furniture you have came from here.'

Agnes (handkerchief to lips): 'Mummy gave us all some furniture when we got married. I think it's an insult that you refused to have her old three-piece suite – I know our Gertrude was upset.'

You (simmering): 'I didn't want any rotten furniture, do you hear me? That suite was so old it probably carried Hannibal over the Alps.'

By now your ulcer's playing up and you've asked Harry to step outside. But then the conversation switches to the money left in a will by the old miser next door who's just snuffed it, and you can see the malice shine on their faces as they recount every gory detail of the miser's demise.

Suddenly, Harry's fallen asleep on the sofa, and the father-in-law's retelling the part he played at Tobruk. Alfred is flourishing the holiday snaps he took at Pontin's two years ago and he's boring the arse off you. The wife's mother, arms akimbo, swells with pride as she motors on about her troubles 'down below', and one of the kids has peed on his Tonka toy. Helplessly, you swing your head about at the sight of domestic hell. Your brain is hot as you look for a chance to escape; your heart is experiencing the Gene Krupa syndrome; this visit has knocked five years off your life.

Mercifully, the day gropes to an end. The family has pulled most of the country to shreds, long-dead relatives have been exhumed and re-slandered, and the boiled ham and tongue lies in a tragic heap in your gut as all the family's complaints are finally aired: 'Dad's liver . . . miracle he's still here.' 'The doctor says my varicose veins have knotted at the back of my knees now.' 'Our Winnie went black on the sofa and said, we'll all meet again in Heaven.' It's not a conversation, it's an organ recital . . . bowels, piles, urinary ducts, wind, periods, no periods, chest congestion, bunions, chilblains, flat feet, green stools, black stools . . . In a lighthearted effort to lift the drama, you intone loudly, 'I've found a way for you to stop losing your hair, Agnes.' The wolf pack glare at you. Agnes is going bald, but it's never mentioned. 'Put it in a box, ha ha ha.' You tail off limply and back away.

Thus endeth the visit and as you drive away with the wife's lips compressed into a thin smouldering line, you know you've had enough. If that chap in the Volvo in front of you doesn't put his foot down . . .

How to Put a Stop to Those Visits

As I hope I have made clear, these dreadful excursions to the in-laws play merry hell with your health. The stress factor alone is sufficient to send you reeling to a rubber farm for deep therapy. (May I suggest Dr Hans Schemmingfester? He's cheap and he's got a lot of cute addresses in Wardour Street.) Something has to be done, but what? Once again, simplicity is the keynote.

Make a discreet visit to your in-laws' locale and pose as an evangelist – one only needs a touch of silver at the temples, steel-rimmed glasses and a Burton suit. Unlike a Jehovah's witness, people seem to unburden themselves to an evangelist, especially if you are adept with a tambourine.

Meet the in-laws' neighbours, go into their homes and sing with them – a Harlem gospel if need be – then casually mention the in-laws and ferret out the extent of their neighbourly relationship. Now is the time to mention that you know a relative of their family . . . you. Say that this relative has just bought a Rolls-Royce for cash and is bringing it along for them to see. Decline a cup of tea and leave rather briskly with a flourish of the tambourine.

It usually takes about two days before the mother-in-law phones up the wife to say that she's heard about the Rolls. Of course your wife is baffled and tells Mummy that it simply isn't true, but clever little you has, prior to this conversation, dropped one or two strange hints to the wife in passing. She will sound a bit odd to her mummy, who in turn will suspect that her daughter is lying through her back teeth and can't wait to flaunt the automobile. Thus the discourse between them will be stilted and strained.

When you hear the telephone receiver crash down on the instrument, creep out of the closet and look as though you've just come in from healing the sick. As your wife asks you about the Rolls-Royce, look puzzled then outraged. Throw your briefcase onto the hall table and stamp one foot – not two, it's a ridiculous fandango and not worthy of an Englishman. Next, slump on the settee and allow the head to hang backwards. This should give you a 'Little Boy Lost' look, which can be most appealing and often brings out the best in a woman – next to a well-stacked wallet, that is.

The dialogue which follows is a wee bit tricky:

You: 'Lordy, what a day I've had. How was yours, my
    love?'
Her: 'Just had mother on the phone. Very odd, she
    sounded.'
You (concerned): 'She isn't having one of her turns, is she?'
Her: 'She said something about you buying a Rolls-Royce.'
You (snap the head forwards): 'What? Is she being
    sarcastic after last week?'
Her: 'How do you mean?'
You: 'I mean about that flare-up I had with Alf over the
    state of my car.'
Her: 'You were a bit tetchy yourself. You did go on.'
You: 'I know I did, love, but your mother always seems to
    take Alf's side and he does rub it in about how well
    he's doing. Sometimes I wonder if you'd have been
    better off with somebody else . . . God knows, I work
    hard enough to provide for you and the kids.'

Her (hopefully this should be the response): 'Don't be silly
– why, you are twice the man Alf is, and I've no
doubts about our life together. I'm surprised at
Mother and her attitude on the phone was peculiar to
say the least. Come to think of it, our Hortense is
getting a bit above herself as well . . . mind you, Agnes
isn't far behind.'

You have created a morass of uncertainty and the family unity
is split. All that remains is to look hurt and puzzled.

You: 'I wish I could afford a Rolls-Royce for us, darling.'
Her: 'You do enough, sweetheart. I've a good mind to tell
Mother what I think of her . . .'
You (hastily): 'The last thing I want is for you and your
mother to fall out over a stupid remark, my angel.'

Her (tenderly): 'You are an old softie, dear. But you're right, I won't ring Mother. I'm not stooping to the family's crass level of humour.'

You: 'Well I must admit I'm more than a little hurt . . .'

Her: 'Don't be, and another thing, we'll stop these weekly visits for a bit. We can start taking the kids out for the day to the seaside now that the weather's improving.'

You've done it, old lad . . . from the horse's mouth, the horror of visiting the old bat is now a thing of the past, for a while at any rate. There will still be a need to fan the flames of suspicion, because when you fail to materialise at the mother-in-law's merry grotto for the ritual visit, she is bound to ring up your wife to see if everything is all right with her and the kids; you could have swamp fever for all she cares. This telephone call must be thwarted, otherwise it could lead to a healing of the family breach and you will have achieved nothing, so now you must take a few days off work and disguise yourself again, this time as a BT lineman.

Clamber up the nearest telephone pole to home, clip into the wire with your own telephone then wait. Answer every call and get accustomed to intercepting them. When the mother-in-law rings, hold a piece of linen to the mouth, and when Mussolini speaks, you say, 'Good morning, madam. Haversham the butler speaking. May I enquire with whom you wish to converse?' This epic lie will stun the old horror for a moment, so forge on in your own voice: 'I'll take the call, Haversham. Pray see if the chauffeur has waxed the Rolls for me, there's a good chap . . . Hello, who is this?' Ten to one she'll bang the receiver down and have a gastric attack.

Not only will this ploy secure you a well-earned breathing space (and bring down the blood pressure as you spend the day normally reserved for the visit lying on the bed for a nap after the pub's closed), it will also stop the jealous sods from coming over to see you.

It is advisable to practise climbing a telegraph pole for at least a week, and do remember to wear sensible clothing and a stout truss.

... and it came to pass that a wife who scolded her husband became known locally as 'Pegasus' because she was the eternal nag.

Her long-suffering husband was dragged to the doctor's by his muscular spouse and she said to the medical chappie: 'There's something wrong with him, doctor, and it's got me worried I don't mind telling you and I've got enough on my plate as it is, God only knows how I cope but cope I do and now this on top of everything else, I'm at my wits' end I tell you and I haven't been well myself but of course I have to carry on and look after the house and pay all the bills my husband has never had a sense of responsibility why I married him I'll never know he's not much but he's all I've got and now he's about to put me in an early grave. Please examine him oh I know he looks well enough but he never seems to hear a word I say to him now what sort of complaint is that, doctor?'

The doctor replied, 'That's not a complaint ... it's a gift.'

We have dealt with major marital problems but we must never overlook the small incidents which can also bring your lifespan to a juddering halt. They may seem trivial, but if allowed to continue, they will render you impotent in your dealings with life. Nagging is one and women thrive on it.

Some years ago, my wife went on and on and on about me buying her a knitting machine. She goaded me to the brink of madness and finally, for the sake of my hearing, I purchased one of the damn things. The noise of the shuttle going up and down drove our cat to strangle himself. There was more wool on the floor than in the average sheep farm, and some of the things she'd knitted would never fit any life-form on this planet. One day she presented me with two sweaters, one blue, one red. I thanked her and put on the blue one to see how it fitted . . .

Wife: 'You don't like the red one, do you?'

Self: 'Why yes, they're both nice, love.'

Wife: 'Well why didn't you put the red one on, then?'

Self: 'No reason, my petal, this was the first one to hand.'

Wife: 'You're so ungrateful, I don't know why I bother.'

Self: 'Okay, sweetheart, I'll put the red one on.'

Wife: 'Don't you patronise me. You don't like it so I'll unpick it.'

Self: 'Bloody hell, woman, I can't wear the two can I? I do like the red one, honestly I do.'

Wife: 'That's the last time I knit anything for you.'

We didn't speak for three days after that, so some good came of it.

The effect of nagging worms into your system. It can spoil your golf swing and make you watch the clock when you're having a drink. The average husband waits with baited breath to see what mood his wife is in, so the tension mounts within and lo . . . the stress factor is back again.

Fortunately, there are many ways to put an end to this problem of nagging. A twelve-bore shotgun, for instance, can work wonders. The only trouble is, where do you bung the body? If you leave it under the floorboards it will smell, if you bury it in the garden that dog next door will scratch it up, and if you hurl it into the sea in a sack, fish will nibble it and add to our pollution.

Divorce? No, that's too costly and ten to one she'll get custody of the car. You could just walk out, I suppose, and live alone on Lundy Island, but then she may meet another bloke and some other poor sod will suffer . . . No, there has to be an alternative – and there is.

How to Make the Wife Give Up Nagging

Hypnosis is the answer. Dr Hans Schemmingfester has devised a method of putting a wife into a trance without actually having to meet her. It's foolproof, believe me; I invested fifty pounds of my own money.

Schemmingfester discovered quite by accident that, if a trumpet is blown at a certain pitch to a woman under hypnosis, she responds to any suggestion given to her. You have to encourage the wife to drive at night, because Schemmingfester fits a small battery-operated pea-bulb to one of the windscreen wipers and when it rains, the wiper goes backwards and forwards and the bulb gives off a little light. The constant movement of the wiper begins the hypnosis. Now place a cassette of a Tibetan flute ensemble playing 'When Irish Eyes are Smiling' into the tape deck of your car radio. There is something about that song when played by Buddhists sitting on their prayer wheels that mesmerises the female, and that, coupled with the pea-bulb, will put her under your control. Speed is now of the essence. Quickly pull out your trumpet and blow a note between the key of F natural and C sharp. Do be careful, one wrong note and you could blow your entire bridgework all over the glove compartment.

The strident trumpet blast will deliver her into your hands completely and the first thing you must do is instruct her to brake the car and stop on the hard shoulder before you have a crash. Then tell her to get out and walk home. She will respond to your orders immediately – if she doesn't then you've wasted money on a rotten trumpet and it could finish up being rammed up your rectum. If successful, you can now drive home alone, park the car, dive into the local pub and proceed to get pissed.

You must carry the trumpet with you at all times, otherwise any small delay in the sequence may bring her round to the level of awareness and you will find yourself in such trouble that only Perry Mason could get you out of it.

Some enterprising husbands have found that if they fit a windscreen wiper on their forehead, with a single-phase motor strapped to the nape of the neck and a fan-belt looped over the ears, plus a small battery taped to the chest to activate the pea-bulb up the nose, they can dispense with taking the wife out at night in the car and put her under the influence anywhere and at any time in the house.

Neighbours can be bothersome if you blow on the trumpet late at night, so sound-proofing is essential for all rooms. Do remember that women are not silly and most of them are as hard as the proverbial nail, so exercise caution in experimenting with your new-found power. If you put her under merely for sex, don't be annoyed if she doesn't move about much during the act; at least she isn't having a headache.

Once you are accustomed to her walking about like a zombie and obeying your every need, life can be fun and there's nothing to stop you having music lessons on the trumpet. One chap who has used the Schemmingfester system for a year now plays the trumpet so well, he gigs at nightclubs with a jazz band and hopes to go on TV's *New Faces* as part of an acrobatic musical team from Sweden.

Some men have written to me asking what would happen if

the tables were turned on them and their wives carried out the Schemmingfester Hypnosis Method ... Fear not, from the moment a man walks to the altar, he is totally under the wife's direction for life. They don't require a pea-bulb or a trumpet for domination: every female is born to power, so let's just thank God we're not spiders, otherwise they'd eat us into the bargain.

Whatever the initial expense of the equipment may be, remember that you will save on new clothes and hairdressing bills once she is under the influence. You need merely say how glamorous she looks and she'll glide away in her vest and

knickers, thinking she's draped in a Paris creation. Thus in one bound we have freed ourselves of a most irritating form of stress induction, and think of the hours you can spend calling her an old bag without the threat of a vase being thrown and imbedded in your head.

You will be stunned, I know, to learn that Christmas is also under scrutiny as a possible stress source, and is of course directly related to nagging as a depressing irritant.

For a married man, Christmas starts as soon as the New Year bustles in. Even before the Easter eggs are in the shops, the average woman is counting the days to the next Yuletide and looking for gifts in mail order catalogues. There was a time when poverty was everyone's middle name and people waited until Christmas Eve before venturing forth to purchase a bird for the table in the hope of getting one cheaper from dealers with a surplus. This practice created towns full of last-minute buyers shouting 'Merry Christmas' to each other and beetling about looking for a bargain . . . Then there was movement and atmosphere; but nowadays, the gifts have been bought and wrapped in readiness as early as October and the pre-frozen turkey has been in the chest freezer for a month.

Just because Christmas falls on the date of a pagan festival, why does Christian doctrine have to mess about with mistletoe and holly? Where does it mention in the Bible about forking out vast sums of cash for electric shavers and aftershave lotions? Let's look at this problem more closely.

Stress in Christmas: Is the Tradition Killing Us?

The first hint of stress comes in making out a list of family and friends who will receive greeting cards and presents. It doesn't matter how many names are put down, ten to one you'll miss out the ones who will send you a card, and that means rushing out to buy more of the confounded things in time for the last Christmas posting date . . . ergo, stress.

Next comes that delightful means of getting into deep financial trouble . . . Who's getting What for a gift. The husband and father is no problem — socks and six white cotton handkerchiefs will do him, plus a pungent phial of aftershave to make him smell like a caretaker from a gay club. When the kids were small, dolls and train sets, puzzles and toys helped a father through the winter months after putting the kids to bed, but now they've grown up and he can't fathom out the computer for the life of him and just how do you regulate that stereo sound-track?

Today's toys cost a lost, but the batteries they need are even more expensive. Somebody in Korea is making a fortune out of you . . .

Every year the wife drones on about buying a real tree for the lounge and of course, quite naturally, new ornaments are required to adorn the damn thing. Don't forget at this stage that fairy lights are needed; the old ones went for a burton when you trod on them under the stairs. Last year my own expenditure on these items ran thus:

Tree: seven foot high Christmas conifer . . . £46.
Decorations: included eight fat glass gnomes, three plastic Father Christmases, tinsel by the furlong, imitation snow,

packaged chocolates and a rather odd fairy for the apex of the tree. Cost? . . . £28.
Small presents for under the tree plus wrapping paper and Sellotape: £12.

Holy cow! I nearly forgot the lights for the tree. Since the year before, they'd shot up in price and
Four strings of fairy lights . . . £34.

The total cost of the tree alone is enough to keep a family of four for a month in Chile. The hallway hasn't been smothered in paperchains yet and Christmas has already set me back £120 smackers.

The house decorations will come to something in the region of £40, and the mountain of Christmas cards can be expected to top £50. It's impossible to estimate how much it will cost you for the wife's present; I leave that sum to you, your bank manager and your defence council.

There's Uncle Harry's gift – why fork out for him? The old sod won't leave you a nickel when he pops his clogs and you once saw him trying to grope Mum. Auntie Ethel from Burslem has been at death's door for so long, it's time somebody pulled her through. She's been hinting at a need for a chiming clock, and one you priced in Selfridges cost more than a second-hand Mini. The mother-in-law, father-in-law, brothers-in-law, sisters-in-law, nieces and nephews will be panting at the door, and on top of the presents you'll have to feed and water the herd into the bargain. Young carol-singers will warble every other ten minutes; at a pound a call, it can mount up over an evening. And don't forget, the kids start carol-singing in late September.

By Christmas Eve, you've no change from about £750, and that is a very low estimate indeed. But it doesn't end there, no by jiminy it doesn't. Have you forgotten the booze and nuts and crisps and puddings? What about the silly bloody crackers?

Come Boxing Day, your intestine has surrendered to the constant supply of turkey and drink, and your liver has a 'For Sale' sign on it. Healthwise you are in a mess: you've got advanced myopia from glaring at the television and you are hoarse from singing all the songs from *The Sound of Music* again. As the bills roll in, the stress of paying for it all will bring the blood pressure up and the ageing process forward.

I agree that when children are small, there is a magic to Christmas, plus the fact that any decent kid will find pleasure in playing with anything; in particular, the boxes his toys arrived in. But is it worth it? How can we avoid this traumatic time of the year?

For an answer, I am indebted to Horace Jollop's book *My Rambles in the Western Desert*. On page seventy-nine, while describing an affair with a riff, Jollop postulates the theory that the best way to avoid the expense of Christmas is by going out and shoplifting three days before it.

Briefly, the idea is to dress in rags, enter a large store and knock off anything that takes your fancy, but make sure the store detective sees you doing it and arrests you before you leave the emporium. At the police station, rant and rave over the economics that have brought you to this parlous state and demand to see a journalist from the *Sun* newspaper (but offer to share any reward for your story with the desk sergeant). Break down and sob on the reporter's shoulder that you have now renounced Christ, Christmas and life. Beg your wife for forgiveness and mention that you love your children, and will think of them while in prison.

Jollop believes that this will bring forth all the do-gooders who will then club together to pay for the things you'd pinched. Church leaders will bring you back into the fold with offers to look after the family at Christmas while you are in the nick. The public outcry over your circumstances will nullify any possibility of a long prison sentence, and while you are in jail the tobacco barons inside will make sure you always have the odd Woodbine. The Government will be under attack over your plight, questions will be asked in the House, and you can sell your story to a women's magazine and retire to Benidorm.

It's worth thinking about even if it means attending gospel meetings for a month or so.

Remember Birthdays and Anniversaries? . . . Forget Them!

Stunning revelation, is it not? Research proves beyond a shadow of a doubt that this awful tradition creates such stress within that it can cause total amnesia. No wonder a man forgets to buy a greetings card or a bunch of wildly over-priced flowers. I can't imagine why we even expect people to remember a birthday; what is the point in celebrating yet another step towards the grave?

I well recall the story of Fred Thrushlebottom, a bachelor who lived with his mother in a Wapping council flat. His devoted mother, year after year, insisted that Fred should celebrate his birthday. The ritual stunted his mental growth, until about two years ago he snapped and raved to his mother:

'NO, Mummy . . . enough is enough! Look at me, I'm fifty-four years of age and you're still asking me to sit on a balloon and burst it with my bottom. You've put trifle and jelly on the table and, as always, some daft kids' entertainer will come round and do tricks. I am *not*, I repeat *not* going to play hide-and-seek in the garage, nor will I indulge in musical chairs any longer. I am a man, Mummy, and that is that, so take the streamers down and cancel the ice cream at once.'

With that, Fred stormed out of the flat and banged the door angrily behind him. Two minutes later, his mother heard a knock on the door. When she opened it, her son Fred was standing there crying bitterly and yelling, 'Mummy . . . I fell!'

By accepting the passing of the years in the celebration of a birthday, we highlight our age. And by being conscious of it, we create stress as the awareness of physical decay looms in our thoughts.

Nevertheless, the one thing that will plummet you into the

very bowels of hell is forgetting to send a bloody card to the wife or failing to mention the great day. You will get the following: first, a silence that will be so solid, you'll be able to cut it out with a putty knife and wear it; second, an in-depth character assassination that will suggest your parents were, in all probability, hybrid hyenas from the Kalahari Desert. You will not be forgiven until your wife has dredged your pockets for a new hat, dress, handbag, hair-do and beauty treatment. My wife is so ugly she doesn't make an appointment to have beauty treatment, she throws out a challenge . . . I once took her to see a horror movie at a local cinema and the audience thought she was making a personal appearance.

To be perfectly fair, my wife isn't really ugly, nor is she very pretty . . . she is, in fact, in between – pretty ugly.

The fortune required to soothe a wife's ruffled feathers is considerable and when you approach the boss for a rise to pay for the loot she's purchased, the nervous system goes haywire when he tells you to sod off. Your body is riddled with strain (giving the ageing process a tremendous boost), and all because you didn't remember to nip out and buy a birthday card. On the other hand, will stress be eliminated if you do remember to get her a card? Not necessarily . . .

> You (handing her the card and a bunch of perky blooms): 'Happy birthday, my darling.'
> Wife (feminine sniff): 'It's not as big as the cards you used to get me.'
> You: 'Sweetheart, it's surely the thought that counts.'
> Wife: 'It must be – certainly wasn't the price, was it? Look for yourself, the price is written in pencil on the back of it.'

It's the Little Things that Irritate

You (livid): 'You are very ungrateful, you really are, the
   price is not the flaming issue here.'
Wife: 'Don't you raise your voice to me! I work my fingers
   to the bone for you: washing, ironing, looking after
   the kids and the house, slaving over that rotten cooker
   – it never was any good. I told you at the time we
   should have gone to the Gas Board, but oh no, you
   had to buy that freak from one of your pals in the
   pub. If you paid me for what I do around here, I'd be
   a millionaire. All I ask is a decent birthday card with
   nice words on . . . Oh and another thing, those
   flowers, did you pinch them from a crypt?'

See what I mean? The next step for you is to stalk out of the
house in a towering rage, crash the gears as you screech the car
out of the drive and narrowly miss side-swiping a lorry as you
fight with the wheel. Stress and more stress . . . But worry no
longer, the Dawson Method will help you to get the wife eating
out of your hand with no expense at all. Before we go any
further, let me assure you that the Dawson Principle is equally
applicable to birthdays and to that other perversity, The
Anniversary.

To forget a wedding anniversary is perhaps the greatest omis-
sion you can ever make. You will never be forgiven for that one
and as the years roll by, the lapse will assume the proportions
of a major tragedy and she, as a woman and a wife, will be the
instrument of your physical and mental decline.
   You must remember that women never forget anything –
they are like elephants, nice to look at but who wants to own
one? They never forget Aunt Ada's anniversary of the time she
had that operation, or Cousin Donald's amputation. They can

recall, without looking it up, little Brenda's birthday or her mother's haemorrhoid removal.

A woman's life is largely made up of dates and data regarding friends and relatives, and she will expect you to be the same. Frankly, I can seldom remember what happened in the pub the night before – mind you, the wife is always telling me about it in detail. So we must be honest with ourselves and realise that we, as mere males, cannot match them in this particular field of human endeavour, therefore we must seek an alternative path to a peaceful and longer life.

My own dear spouse has the strongest jaw known to medical science. I made the fatal mistake of overlooking our tenth wedding anniversary, and she was still ranting about it on our fifteenth. I completely forgot our twentieth anniversary, but while she looked about for a suitable weapon a divine inspiration came to me. I offer it to you freely. As she drew back her arm in readiness to hurl the teapot, I delivered this eulogy:

'Yes, my precious, I did forget our anniversary, and I forgot it on purpose. Because I love you dearly, I subconsciously pine for time to stand still for ever and a day.

'Encapsulated in my heart, beloved, is the memory of our wedding day. As we stood at the altar with the rays of the warm August sun filtering through the stained glass windows and dappling the Saxon majesty of the church into fragmented loveliness, I saw your translucent beauty shimmering in your white dress of purity. For me, that moment became a shrine in my every waking thought.

'I need no constant yearly reminder of our life together; there is no passage of time, darling heart. You are as beautiful now as you were then when we pledged our souls to each other.

'How can I think to indicate your age by the folly of sending you a birthday card? Time for you has stopped and that is how I see you, darling, always the young girl with shining eyes, the girl who gave herself to me, unworthy person that I am.

'By not appearing to remember such things, thus do I remember them more clearly. There is not a moment when I don't utter a silent prayer to Our Maker for allowing me to share your life, my own true love ... Anniversary and birthday cards are for those who will never know what real passion is, because that passion is in the heart. Why should I demean your loveliness by proffering flowers? There has never been a bloom yet that could complement your inherent flawless beauty. A flower is dross when compared to you, my lovely.'

When I'd finished speaking, I saw that she had put the teapot back on the draining board, and that even as she said, 'Bullshit', her eyes were moist and tender.

From that moment on, I have never had to worry about remembering her birthday or our anniversary, and if unkind people say to her, 'Hasn't the miserable git got you anything?' my wife looks at me lovingly and croons, 'We don't need material artifacts to show what we feel for each other, do we, dearest?' That usually shuts the buggers up, and they don't mention seeing me being carried out of the pub. They assume, from what she has said, that she already knows about the incident and condones it.

A lot of my pals have adopted the Dawson Principle and they all swear that they feel much better, physically and mentally. It is wise to throw poetic ramblings to the wife in between birthdays and anniversaries, and a ploy I have used on occasion is to make sure that she is listening as I pick up the phone, dial a non-existent number and say loudly, 'No George, I am not going to the pub tonight, I'm having an evening with my wife – she's more important to me than drinking with that rabble.'

... and so it came to pass that a man wanting to do some house extension work went to see his bank manager. Nervously he walked into the bank, feeling about as comfortable as a stripper with grit in her G-string.

The bank manager shook him warmly by the throat and then hopped into his office. He had to, the man was kissing his feet at the time.

The man sat down and the manager said, 'Before we can discuss a loan, have you got collateral?'

The man said, 'No, it's the way my legs are crossed.'

The bank manager droned on and on: 'You've been coming into this branch for over seven years now asking for money, and in all that time you've never noticed that I've got a glass eye.'

The man said, 'It's your left one.'

The bank manager said, 'How did you know?'

The man replied, 'It's the only one with a spark of humanity in it.'

Yes my friend, this one can take years off your life and it's mainly women who are responsible for it.

You have a nice semi-detached home and you can afford the mortgage quite comfortably if you don't eat or clothe yourself. For a couple of years everything has been fine and dandy, until a new neighbour moves in and starts to Do Things to his property. Naturally, you're invited in for coffee, and of course the coffee break includes a look around the house with a résumé of what they intend to do.

Suddenly your spouse becomes restless and there are long silences between you when the kids have been bundled off to bed and their computers. As a mere male, you wonder what is amiss and it will be you who brings up the question . . .

Husband: 'Er, is everything all right, dear?'

Wife: 'Suppose so.'

Husband: 'You seem strangely perturbed, my petal. Is there anything I can do?'

Wife: 'It's the kitchen for one thing – there isn't room in there to swing a tapeworm, let alone a cat.'

Husband: 'You have never complained before.'

Wife: 'I've bitten my tongue a few times, I can tell you. I bark my shins every time I open the cupboard doors, and there isn't room for the microwave oven . . . Oh, I could go on and on.' [And of course she will.]

Husband: 'You liked it when we bought the house, in fact you said it was the best feature.'

Wife: 'I knew you liked the house and I didn't want to seem ungrateful, dearest, because I knew you had your heart set on it – and also of course we couldn't afford the one I wanted.'

Husband: 'Well damn it all . . .'

Wife: 'Don't swear, you're not a Liberal. I'm merely saying that the kitchen just isn't big enough and the ceiling is so low the only fish I can fry is plaice. They had the same sort of kitchen next door but they've done marvels with it, marvels I tell you . . . Mind you, by the looks of it they can well afford it.'

Now of course you've got your back up and she knows it. The seeds of envy have been sown, and you feel like a squatter. You decide to show that so-and-so next door that anything he can do you can do better, and your fate is sealed.

First, you have to get somebody in to design the alteration. The wife will suggest a visit to a kitchen centre and naturally enough they will produce someone who will, for a trifling sum, draw up plans for the proposed new kitchen. This 'someone' was, in all probability, lurking behind an Aga assessing how much he could screw you for. The die is cast; soon a bright man arrives at the door and out comes a tape measure and a box of pencils and he crows to your wife that he'll provide a first class drawing of the proposed changes.

A few days later, he will deliver a set of plans that makes Coventry Cathedral look like a sauna shed, and with it a bill for seventy-five pounds for the drawing. (If you live south of Watford, the bill will be in excess of a hundred and forty pounds.) The kitchen centre people are most obliging; they know a *very* good builder who can't wait to start work for such a charming couple, and sure enough, one morning a florid artisan introduces himself as Mr —— the builder. Your wife will flutter around him as he ponderously weighs up the task ahead.

'Piece of cake,' he'll say confidently, 'straightforward job.'

That is the moment when you should show him the door and say you're going to excavate in Chile for a month.

One morning soon afterwards – and you can bet it will be a bad one – several sullen workmen will appear with the intention of knocking seven bells out of the kitchen. They will have dust-sheets that never stop the muck from settling everywhere, they will have planks and trestles, hammers, axes and drills and, of course, very large brew cans.

Within three days, the noise will be driving you to the abyss of insanity and your nerves will be as frayed as last year's cardigan. The dust from the fallen débris will get on your chest and the wife will start rubbing your back with Vick Vapour

Rub. Don't make the fateful mistake I did by asking them if they'd like a cup of tea. In days of yore before the modern health kick, one simply brewed a pot of Massawattee with milk and sugar . . . not any more.

You: 'Like a cuppa, lads?'
1st man: 'Weak for me, no milk, half a sugar.'
2nd man: 'Strong, preferably herbal, no sugar and dried milk extract.'
3rd man: 'Earl Grey with lemon and sweeteners, failing that Malvern Water.'
Apprentice: '7-Up please or Marmite . . . any Coke?'

You can't sleep because your ears are still throbbing with the day's din. When you do drop off, you wake up coughing plaster dust from your aching and overburdened lungs, and the wife's voice starts drilling into your head with ideas for what sort of new units she wants.

The next blow to depress the spirit comes when the workforce in the kitchen solemnly intone that the job is going to be more difficult than they first thought. Out cometh the builder, only this time the pompous and hearty gentleman wears a frown and avoids your eyes. He talks in a sepulchral boom: 'Yes, well, you need a girder across so-and-so . . . Didn't estimate for that on the original price. Dampness everywhere, needs to be seen to . . . Cost, well, ha ha, price of things today, what?'

You are now being heavily screwed and there isn't a damn thing you can do about it. A vision of your bank manager's face drifts before your eyes and your bowels turn to mush.

With renewed vigour, knowing full well that they have you by the scrotum, the workmen gleefully demolish the interior and you have to go and lie down. Healthwise, as our American cousins would say, you are heading for a coroner's report, and all because the lady wants a bigger kitchen.

Weeks drag by, the workmen are still at it, and you have started talking to yourself in the broom cupboard. Quite a heap of dandruff mantles your shoulders these days and you have developed a nervous eye tic. You grin mirthlessly at the wall and you won't answer the telephone. You've taken to creeping into the bank in disguise to cash a cheque and you are convinced that a detective is following you.

The wife is blooming and can't wait to pull you along to the kitchen centre to select the next phase of your impending bankruptcy: the new fitted units.

The first thing to remember is that the cost is astronomical and you may need seriously to contemplate an armed raid on Barclays. There will be steel units, pine units, Olde Worlde units, and units with marble tops . . . There will be a breathtaking collection of suitable tiles for the floor, tiles for the walls, dishwashers, washing machines and awe-inspiring waste disposal fittings . . . There will be walk-in freezers large enough to store a cow, built-in hobs and double ovens . . . It's a sort of technical Disneyland, and they all cost just under the price of a Concorde engine.

The wife will have to be lifted bodily out of the centre, frothing with desire and excitement – and you, my friend, will have to sell your soul to pay for it all. The stage is set for your physical and mental decay: so the question is, how do you avoid this pitfall in the first place?

As soon as the wife starts to moan about an extension, don't put up a defence – agree with her immediately. This ploy will throw her off the scent and enable you to work out a scheme to thwart her. Then visit a seedy theatrical agent, of whom there are many . . . mine included. You'll find their offices are usually in a condemned tenement block behind a gas works.

The agent will of course fawn over you, and offer a selection of acts who haven't appeared in public since Dunkirk. You must harden your heart to his blandishments and very firmly tell him what you are looking for, which is an out-of-work Shakespearean actor with a knowledge of local history . . . (This last point is important.) For a trifling sum and the promise of a practical pie, you should obtain one quite easily, if you know which pub he drinks in.

At home, enthuse with the wife over her ideas for the bigger kitchen and casually mention that you've heard that the *Antiques Roadshow*, BBC-2's popular programme, is in the area and people are being approached to go on it with artifacts. Ten to one, the wife's ears will prick up and she'll eagerly rush to the attic to bring out her grandmother's Edwardian chamberpot, which she is fully convinced is worth a fortune. Stagger back when you see it and say that you will now find out more for her satisfaction. Don't mention any further plans to approach the BBC for at least a week, then hide the chamberpot until she realises that it's missing. (Incidentally, don't be tempted to use it – it could take the glaze off and lower the value.) When she asks in a worried tone what's happened to it, raise your head from the sketches of the kitchen extension that you've been doodling on, allow an expression of wonderment to glide across your features and say, 'Darling, I nearly forgot! I took the pottie along to a BBC outside broadcasting unit in the High Street and left it with them. The producer said he'd let me know.'

Be prepared for the wife to go berserk. She'll rant on about how much that pisspot meant to her family, and how it should never have been left with strangers – you know, the usual thing. When she flounces out dabbing her eyes, signal with a lantern from the window that it is time for the actor to pay his call. When he presses the bell, shout loudly, 'I'll get it, my beloved.' Then take the pot from its hiding place and as you open the door, place it in the actor's hands.

'Darling, have you got a minute?' you yell to your spouse, and when she hoves into view, introduce him as Cranberry Standhome, the BBC's expert on pottery. Ideally, the actor should be tall with long flowing grey hair and wearing a cape. As per rehearsal, he will kiss the back of her hand, hold aloft the chamberpot, and boom, 'Madam, pray forgive this intrusion into your domicile, but in truth, fair lady, I simply had to confront the possessor of this magnificent fundamental utensil.'

Before the wife can ask how much the thing is worth, the actor must carry on thus: 'This house . . . this jewel of suburbia . . . What architect of mortal clay could possibly have designed such contours?'

As the wife simpers and pats her hair, allow the actor to roam unchecked from the living room to the kitchen, where he must pause dramatically before he speaks the next lines: 'God's blood . . . That I should, this darkling night, feast my orbs upon such a creation of craftsmanship and feminine good taste . . . A welding of imagination – and 'tis a tone poem, is it not – a cultural oasis in a mindless orbit.'

The wife's mouth should be so agape, it resembles the rim of a wet bucket . . .

Wife: 'Thank you. Actually, my husband and I have been thinking of extending it.'
Actor: 'WHAT? Infamy, I say . . . How can you extend

beauty? Oh that I should hear this barbaric diatribe
. . . Extend it? Never, dear lady.'

The wife will be a little dumbstruck, but if the actor plays the
rôle as if he was auditioning for *Brookside* she'll find herself
quivering with uncertainty.

> Wife: 'Well, er, thank you . . . but don't you think the
>   kitchen is too small as it is?'
> Actor: 'S M A L L? S M A L L? Did shortness prevent Tom
>   Thumb from achieving world renown?'
> Wife: 'Well . . .'
> Actor: 'Of course it didn't . . . Look at Napoleon, had
>   Europe on its knees and he was only five foot four.'
> Wife: 'Yes but . . .'
> Actor: 'Beauty is small, my sweet one. May I be so bold as
>   to utter that your natural loveliness would have been
>   marred had you been taller?'

That should do it. Pat the wife on the back, reaffirm what the
thespian has just said, and then pay him off in soiled readies.

From that day forth, she will scoff at people who go in for
extending their homes. Some may ponder as to why she has a
smile on her face when a neighbour shows her the new kitchen
or bedroom, and think that you as a husband must have an
incredible sexual allure.

Actors for Consideration

Humphrey Pyke: Aged forty-three, bald with own teeth. Has
played Hamlet in the Polperro Theatre of the Macabre, and
once did a walk-on in the television production of *Rainbow*.

Stanislau Thorningham: Aged thirty-eight, from Oldham. Can whistle in Polish and climb into a catsuit for pantomimes. Was in the series *Upstairs, Downstairs*. You didn't see him because when the cameras were upstairs, he was down.

Mainwaring Grimethorpe: Aged fifty-nine and a bit. Played a French maid in a club frolic in Polynesia, and is wanted by the Dutch Secret Police. At present appearing in a nude version of *Gone with the Wind* at the Cocoa Rooms and Thermal Baths, Crewe.

. . . and it came to pass that a man put his house up for sale. One night a chap called and the following conversation ensued . . .

'Good evening, can I help you?'

'I've called with the object of purchasing your house,' said the visitor. 'I'm new to the area, I'm Irish.'

'O really?'

'No, O'Donovan.'

'You've got a lot of medals on your chest – have you been on the front?'

'Yes, but I couldn't get any answer so I came round the back . . . Tell me, have you got dry rot?'

'No, it's the way I'm standing,' replied the householder.

'Did you decorate yourself?'

'No, I put it on the walls.'

If you thought that smoking and drinking were bad for you, try looking for a house. I sincerely guarantee that after viewing about half a dozen houses for sale, you will have developed a headache and blurred vision, not to mention nervous tension and abdominal irritation.

Let us ponder on the fate of a couple I knew very well. In case of a lawsuit, we shall call them Mr and Mrs Pilgrim.

They had enjoyed two years of connubial bliss, living with Mr Pilgrim's parents, when his wife began to hint that it was time for them to leave the family nest and find a place of their own. Mr Pilgrim didn't relish the idea of leaving Mummy and Daddy – after all, it was costing him considerably less than a home of his own, and it was handy for the pub. But as well we know, the force of the female tongue is greater than the power of a fleet of Cruise missiles, and so our intrepid duo set off upon the self-destructive path of ownership.

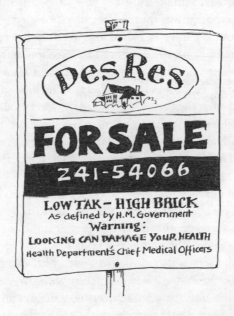

Their very first port of call was the office of an estate agent. Now if you've never had dealings with an estate agent, allow me to enlighten you about this most appalling of professions. Remember that they have the imagination of Jules Verne and Conan Doyle and the ruthless streak of a Mongolian cavalry-man. They write in a language which is a sort of defunct Yiddish, for example: 'For sale. Mod com sem det, fit kit, dub gadge, excel gads, rural asp.' This, as any scholar versed in obscure dead languages will tell you, means simply: 'For sale.

Modern comfortable semi-detached. Fitted kitchen, double garage, excellent gardens and rural aspect.' But when you go to view it, the description will seem strangely at odds with what you actually see. Oh, it's a semi-detached all right, but the other half is a disused slaughterhouse. The kitchen is fitted with a sink and a wooden top that is liberally sprinkled with mouse shit. The double garage is a shed and in truth, it *would* fit two cars . . . one on top of the other. The excellent gardens are a blaze of colour . . . dirty brown, and the soil is so hard, you would have to blast holes in it with a submachine-gun to plant seeds. Mark you, the beds are so small, flowers would grow up round-shouldered. At the front the garden measures four feet by three and, although the rear patch is bigger by two foot six inches, that is for the manhole cover which conceals a reeking culvert that has been blocked since V E-day.

The flight of fancy soars to new dimensions when it comes to the words 'rural aspect'. From the lounge window, there is a panoramic view of an adventure playground for disturbed infantile thugs, and if you crane your head to the left of the playground, there is a tree of sorts with filth carved into the rotting bark. From the bedroom front window you can just make out the bulk of an engineering works, and on a still morning you can clearly hear the oaths of a strike picket having breakfast.

Meanwhile, our friends Mr and Mrs Pilgrim sallied forth clutching the information sheet supplied by the estate agent. Their first call was at number 22, Rose Petal Avenue. It sounded fair dinkum: '22 Rose Petal Avenue, a split level bungalow of great charm. Will need a little work on it.'

Number 22 Rose Petal Avenue was in a cul-de-sac and it was split level all right – one half of it was level, the other half was split. A recluse lived in it but admitted under pressure that he was in fact a squatter since the real owner had perished from rat bites. The little work needed included a new lavatory and bath, a roof and some doors putting back, once new wooden jambs had been fitted. Price? A trifling one hundred and twenty-seven thousand pounds and free consultation with Rentokil.

Slightly jaundiced, the Pilgrims drove off to another house for sale, this time under the colourful heading 'Superlative mock-Tudor dwelling, detached with indoor swimming pool'. The house made a mockery of the Tudor period; it was actually a Gothic slum built as an asylum for mad orphans. It wasn't really detached, some of the joists still clung to the house next door, and the swimming pool was a sunken iron tank that had fallen through the floor. The tank's original purpose was obscured by the mists of time, but a retired librarian with angina told Mrs Pilgrim that, in her opinion, it had been used to scald confessions out of heretics.

By now the Pilgrims were confused and wearied by the web of deceit in which they had been cocooned, and Mrs Pilgrim wanted to go for a pee. Depressed but unbowed, the Pilgrims safaried on in search of a brick-built Shangri-La, this time with the aid of another estate agency . . .

'Has to be Seen to be Believed! Unusual six-storey Dwelling with Sea Views . . . a snip at one hundred and forty-eight thousand pounds.' The Pilgrims found that this was an old lighthouse with the top bitten off. It stood on a pile of rocks near Southport, and the sea hadn't come in for centuries. As Mrs Pilgrim remarked sourly, 'It would have cost too much for a stair carpet.'

'Quasi Semi Surrounded by Woodlands', said another sheet. This turned out to be a pre-fab in the middle of a timber yard, and the roof was so low, only Quasimodo could have walked under it.

'Olde Worlde Cottage in Unusual Setting', read the Pilgrims. 'Unusual setting' was accurate . . . the cottage was in a back street in Lambeth. A building which had started out as a tenement now had black-painted wooden strips down its grimy walls with plastic ivy glued to them. At this stage Mrs Pilgrim had to be treated for a minor breakdown by a paramedic, and Mr Pilgrim's piles started to play up again.

'Executive House in Ten Acres of Land' sounded more promising. But the executive must have been an accountant for the Mafia. The windows were barred, and the house was so far off the beaten track, Dracula got in for the SDP. Mr Pilgrim couldn't help noticing bullet holes in the stone façade, and then realised that the ten acres the house stood in were part of the Bisley Rifle Range. Mrs Pilgrim had been admitted to a nursing home by now, and kept telling the staff that she was the real Prince Philip.

Mr Pilgrim struggled on alone. In quick succession, he inspected a property glowingly described as a 'Detached House off the Great North Road'. God only knows what road the agent was referring to, as the nearest town was Oslo. He then glanced at a house that was so damp the guttering was on the inside and the owner confessed that he'd had to have his furniture undersealed.

Finally, broken in spirit and health, the couple settled for a ground floor flat which was close to a hospital for Mrs Pilgrim to visit daily in her bath chair. Mr Pilgrim had gone bald with worry and now wears an absurd wig. The bags under the poor chap's eyes are so big he's started carrying them around in a golf trolley . . . All that, just because the lady wanted a home of her own.

How to Avoid Buying Property

You might say that they should have gone in for a new house – well, have you looked at what passes for building and architecture today? The rooms are so tiny, when you turn the light off you're in bed before it's dark. Some of them are so jerry-built, you pay your rates in Berlin. Most of them are situated on vast estates with walls so thin, if the wife uses a steam iron, next door's wallpaper peels off. For the price of one of them, you could cheerfully retire to Jamaica with a couple of concubines.

Don't forget that getting a mortgage is an exercise in torment. Like bank managers, building societies will only be ready to lend you money providing you can prove you don't need it. I went to one once and I said to the manager, 'How do I stand for a mortgage?' He replied, 'Son, you don't stand . . . you grovel.'

The next person to send you reaching for an open razor is of course that pin-stripe-suited barracuda the solicitor, who will cheerfully take over the piffling business of 'conveyancing'. Expect to put your hand in your pocket for another tidy sum. Whoever said, 'Put your money in bricks and mortar'? If things get rough financially, I can't see a bank accepting a lintel as a payment off your overdraft.

It doesn't matter a jot if the place you've bought is new or pre-Boer War, buying a house is trouble. Of course we have to live in something, I suppose; living in a cave could give you a lime rash and the council wouldn't like it. The problems of sanitation in a cave could dampen your enthusiasm, especially during a prolonged summer, and there is nowhere to dress for dinner. You might, if pushed, live in a tent in the manner of a Romany tinker but you'd be hard pressed to find enough room for the youngster's Scalectrix. Keep away from caravans –

people will hand you pans to be soldered and you have to push the damn thing to and fro when the wife is on the loo.

So what is the answer to this dire and often anguishing dilemma? Allow me, if you will, to use my experience to guide you in the method that dropped a house in my lap for nothing . . . I married a wonderful girl, but her mother wasn't and in that I was extremely fortunate. For what I had to do, I needed enmity so that my conscience wouldn't keep me up at nights reading a back copy of *Playboy*.

Quite frankly, the wife's mother and I did not see eye to eye, mainly because she was nine inches taller than I. She used to snort to her neighbours that I was effeminate. . . . Mind you, compared to her, I was.

Physically she was a big woman with a lot of the things that men desire . . . muscles and a duelling scar. She was so fat she didn't have elastic in her knickers, she had a Swish track fitted . . . When she passed her handbag from one hand to the other, she threw it. She tried joining Weight Watchers but every time she went to a meeting they pulled the blinds down. I've never seen a female who was so enormous, in fact she had to get her brassière on prescription. She bent down once in Liverpool to adjust her stockings, and they had an eclipse in Bournemouth. During the last war, she was asked to float on her back to fool the Germans, and it worked . . . they bombed her thinking she was the Isle of Wight. The French Army wanted to give her a medal for gallantry, but they couldn't find a general who'd kiss her.

I'm not saying for a moment that she was ugly, but I used to pin a photograph of her over the mantelpiece to keep the kids away from the fire. I looked at it this way: if beauty is indeed skin deep, then she was going through life inside out. She went to the zoo one memorable day and I had to buy two tickets, one to get her in and one to let her out. As she was walking past the monkey mountain, a rampant gorilla leapt on her and started ripping her clothes off. She screamed to her husband, 'Bert, what should I do?' and my father-in-law, in a rare moment of raw courage, replied, 'Do what you always do ... tell him you've got a headache.'

This, then, was the woman I had to live with when her daughter and I first got married because we could not, under any circumstances, buy a home of our own. My parents hadn't got any room in their house – it was a tiny council dwelling, just one bedroom, on an estate that was so tough, the youngster across the road shot his mum and dad so he could go on an orphans' picnic.

From the moment I set foot in my mother-in-law's house, I was under martial law and a curfew. The house was decorated in early Gestapo and my hostess had a jackboot rash. The only time I was permitted to open my mouth was when I yawned, and every time she saw me, my face lit up ... she used to ram my nose up a lamp socket.

One night an idea came to me, as she wrestled me to the carpet in a half-nelson. She had a fear of ghosts. Why she had this phobia I'll never know, but probably she was haunted by the memories of her victims in Prussian slave camps. The plan was simple ... I contacted a friend of mine who knew the brother of a lady whose aunt was a spiritualist. Madame De Vere-Smythe was her name and she was about as genuine as a Renoir done in ball-point, but she looked the part.

Despite her prim and proper approach to life, the wife's mother enjoyed her gin and tonics after a night at bingo, so I arranged for Madame De Vere-Smythe, alias Elsie Midgeland, to be present in the pub that the female Martin Bormann frequented. To give credit where credit is due, Madame was quite magnificent. As the mother-in-law was on her fourth large one, and beginning to relate stories of Luftwaffe tactics, Madame De Vere-Smythe leant across and hushed the entire pub as she intoned in a voice from beyond: 'There is an evil spirit that abides within your home, my dear lady ... a Creature from the Pit.'

Naturally the wife's mother looked straight at me, but paled when Madame went on: 'Protest if you will ... but you are afraid of the Unknown.' The expression on the wife's mother's face was worth every penny of the twenty-five quid demanded by Madame De Vere-Smythe.

The upshot was that my mother-in-law agreed to allow Mrs Midgeland (I mean, of course, Madame De Vere-Smythe) to hold a séance in the house to exorcise the malignant spirit knocking about the place. Seated at the walnut dining table were Madame, myself, the mother-in-law and the father-in-law. The wife washed her hands of the whole affair and went off to her aerobics class where they do peculiar things with the pelvis. On a whispered instruction, the lights above the table were dimmed, we held hands and the farce began ...

'Is there anybody here from the Other World?' whispered Madame. Nothing happened apart from the father-in-law breaking gentle wind. Madame tried again: 'There is a presence in this room ... who are you?'

The wife's mother was agitated; I could hear her corsets scraping on the vinyl-padded chair. (If she had put on any more weight, she'd have had to discard the corsets and start wearing baling wire.)

Suddenly, I felt Madame's knee deliberately bang the underside of the table. 'Aha!' she cried. 'You are here ... who are you?'

The silence was intense and I saw Madame twist the corner of her mouth in preparation for imitating a voice. (I should add, at this dramatic point, that Madame toured the halls for many years as a lady ventriloquist and could throw her voice quite passably – although when she did, it sounded a bit like Donald Duck.)

Madame: 'I am the spirit of the Great Ram, Lord of the Nile, a Prince of Darkness.'

The wife's mother screamed out loud and yelled, 'Tell 'im to piss off.'

Madame: 'Be quiet! What do you want, Great Ram?'

Voice: 'Justice, for my death . . . I demand blood for blood' (long pause while Madame adjusted her teeth) 'I go . . . I go.'

Madame shook her head and droned, 'I couldn't hold him back . . . Put on the lights.'

The mother-in-law was ashen. 'Have you got rid of him, Madame Smith?'

Madame shuddered and replied acidly, 'It's Smythe, dearie, not Smith. No, I haven't got rid of him, there is something in this house that keeps his spirit imprisoned for all time.'

The mother-in-law said suspiciously, 'Why hasn't he made contact before now? We've lived here for twenty-two years.'

That stumped Madame for a while, then she recovered her composure and said, 'The wheels of the Other World turn slowly, my dear. Question not . . .'

Only one step was left before my Master Plan was complete . . . the hiring of a Balkan lady of ill repute to get an electronics engineer into a compromising situation in a boarding house, in order for me to take photographs and blackmail him into putting some equipment into the mother-in-law's home. My victim was a wretched ex-Ferranti boffin married to a limbo dancer who had a lot of shares in Woolworth's.

He fell for the Balkan whore and dropped like a ripe peach into my waiting paws. I took many photographs that amply demonstrated the imagination of a sex-starved suburbanite with a willing Jugoslav trollop ... although the snap of him jumping off the wardrobe in a wet suit was an exercise in bad taste.

He paled at the blackmail threat, broke into the mother-in-law's house and secreted small speakers in her bedroom. These were wired to a secret passage behind the kitchen in which I was seated before a microphone.

The rest is history. I moaned in a deep voice every night for a week and rattled chains, and the wife's mother packed her bags and fled to the Azores. The father-in-law thanked me, drew his money out of a Post Office Special Investment account, and bought a pub in Newmarket ... Thus the house was mine; no mortgage to pay and I let out the attic bedroom to help pay the rates. The only slight snag was the wife. One night in a fit of pique after learning that her mother had joined the Baader-Meinhof gang, she ran off with the chap next door – and I must confess, I do miss him.

So there is the method for securing a home without buying it. Simply endure a time with the in-laws and wait for weaknesses.

Should you feel that my scheme is a better one than wholesale slaughter, drop me a line, hopefully attached to some cash, and I'll give you the address of Madame De Vere-Smythe, who is now blackmailing me. The Balkan trollop is available for hire, subject to my commission of course.

How to Give Up Gardening

. . . and it came to pass that Mr Potter was awarded First Prize for his vegetable garden, and well deserved too, the man's neighbours said. Mr Potter spent all his available time on his garden, and it was a joy to behold.

One day, a tramp passing the bottom of Mr Potter's garden felt the urgent need to evacuate his bowels, and as time was of the essence, he climbed over Mr Potter's fence, removed his trousers and dumped. Being a neat sort of chap he looked down with the intention of burying the débris . . . Lo! No sign of his evacuation. Odd, he thought and he walked away puzzled.

Two days later, he returned and saw Mr Potter doing something with his marrows, so he said, 'Excuse me, sir, you have a lovely garden – nobody ever trespasses on it, do they?'

Mr Potter replied, 'Not really, it's quiet round here – but I'd like to get my hands on the person who shat on my son's tortoise.'

Some readers may be surprised at the inclusion of gardening as 'something that is bad for you'. But to anybody who has strived to find a decent gardener, its insertion will come as no profound shock.

For a long time I searched for a house with a fairly large garden in the misguided belief that I would eventually become a sort of weekend Percy Thrower. In my mind's eye, I saw myself motoring home to potter about grandly with a hoe, ready to prod dreamily at things poking up amid a sea of landscaped lawns and swaying shrubs.

The first time I set eyes on the garden I'd inherited, I thought I was looking at a film set for *Day of the Triffids*. I don't know who had owned the garden before me, but it must have been someone who'd fallen in love with a Congolese rain forest. For a start, the grass was so tall, every time a frog jumped to peer over it, he got a double hernia . . . and such was the state of the fish-pond, whenever I threw a stone into its turgid depths, the smell that emerged was positively mauve.

In every direction weeds could be seen throttling one another, and so dense was the undergrowth around the invalid trees, I was afraid of being attacked by a wild pig. Every time I trudged through the tangled wilderness I stepped into something awful, and the probability of a cholera outbreak became a daily fear.

I tried setting fire to it all, but the wind changed direction. The gazebo burnt down and the kitchen was gutted.

For weeks I dug up old pottery, bricks, cement blocks, animal bones, an abandoned sofa, the top of a gas cooker and something that looked like the remains of a First World War submarine.

Three times in one daylight onslaught I fell into the accursed fish-pond and I swear that, on each occasion, something underneath the surface tried to pull me to the bottom. I hacked at, chopped at, sawed at, hammered at the dead clump of geriatric elms, but they fought back and blistered my hands, wrenched my spine into a knotted rhapsody of pain, and poked several branches through the windscreen of our Mini.

The damned garden had beaten me, and I found myself spending hours waving my fist at it through the lounge window. The kids were muttering about 'having dad seen to', whatever that meant, and some of the older neighbours took to making the sign of the cross when they spotted me. I think perhaps I was becoming slightly deranged. Obviously this state of affairs couldn't continue, otherwise Daddy would find himself in a linen shift being interviewed by a serious chap in a white coat.

Thanks to the local free press, just before breaking point was reached I espied an advertisement: 'For a garden to be proud of, contact the Specialist Landscaping and Gardencare Company'. I telephoned them and a most agreeable voiced young lady assured me that the Specialists would make a visit the following day. I felt that a tremendous weight had been lifted from my shoulders and I ran into the jungle that was mine own, crying aloud, 'Your days are numbered, tomorrow you all die.' I raised my head and brayed to the moon, stepped back too sharply, stumbled into the fish-pond and struggled with the tentacles of the something unimaginable that lay in wait.

The grey bars of the morrow stretched across the sky and I stood by the window, nose pressed against the glass, eagerly awaiting the arrival of the Specialist Landscaping and Gardencare Company. At approximately 10.15 a.m. a resplendently rusty truck puffed into the driveway, and out clambered three short men in green overalls carrying the sort of sinister equipment usually associated with Inca ritual tortures. I trotted towards them and I think, looking back, that they were abashed when I kissed their outstretched hands.

They stood for an eternity gazing at the garden and shaking their noble heads as they surveyed the mess. Remarks like 'Wot a bloody sight', and 'Christ almighty, does Tarzan live 'ere?' were among the printable ones uttered. At a given signal, brew cans appeared and were silently handed to me. Looking over my shoulder as I sped to the business of tea distillation, I saw them sprawl on the ground with pipes and cigarettes already ignited.

After tea and sandwiches, plus a careful scrutiny of the Page
Three nude, the trio dragged themselves behind the truck, and
didn't reappear until twelve noon. Then with a considerable
effort they moodily entered the green hell and the sound of
sporadic labour drifted out – until 12.45 p.m., when they
tottered out with brew cans at the ready.

Work, if you will excuse the term, recommenced at 2.36 p.m.
and soon flames were clearly visible coming from the undergrowth. Like me, they misinterpreted the direction of the
capricious wind, and this time it was part of the dining room
that went.

My wife had long since lost her grip on reality, and had been
taken to an understanding relative in the Lake District.

At the end of the week, and with the help of more Specialist
Landscaping staff, my garden resembled the aftermath of the
Somme. Nothing stirred out there any more . . . all that could
be seen was a half acre of black charcoal and smouldering
funeral pyres. It was a hollow victory, for in committing
genocide on the garden, I had made the gazebo a memory in
white ash, the kitchen an ebony shell, the dining room a
scorched ruin – and the bill was for so much money, it could
have saved the economy of Uganda.

It was time for the Grand Reconstruction. I haunted garden
nurseries and paled at the expense of shrubs and bushes, trees
and plants. I cleaned out the fish-pond and, with the help of a
very nice man who did odd jobs, I made it bigger as a main
feature. Then I discovered the price of fish to put in it. One
lunatic demanded seventy pounds for a brightly coloured
goldfish . . . seventy pounds, I swear. Marine life would have to
wait until some peculiar uncle in Tasmania left me a bundle.

Quite suddenly, the very nice man who did odd jobs quit the

area. I went through some very odd job men after that. One
elderly churl agreed to assist me for a king's ransom. He was a
tall thin man who sighed heavily and frequently, and constantly blew his purple nose on a sheet of newspaper. He would
pick up a shovel, sigh, let the tool fall by its own momentum,
then bend down and look to see if he'd left any marks. I found
him in a semi coma clutching a bottle of rum behind the privet,
chewing on my son's pet tortoise and crying, 'The crust on this
pie's too hard.'

Purely by my own efforts the garden was beginning to take
shape but the backache, the long stints with fork and spade, the
legs quivering with fatigue . . . I had to find somebody to ease
the burden, and another Odd Jobby arrived in answer to my ad
in the local tabloid. He was young and built like a water-
buffalo in labour. Here's my man, thought I, as he flexed the
enormous lumps on his arms and started pushing the mower
across the greensward. One minute later he stopped and
minced over to a group of gladioli, plucked one and kissed it.
His outrageous biceps, the size of a Sumo wrestler's thighs,
bulged as he ran his fingers through his long curly blond hair,

previously hidden under his flowing hat. He saw me peering at him and mouthed a kiss in my direction.

The following day, he had in tow a slim wan young man in yellow skin-tight matador pantaloons and a bright sweater that was a woollen nightmare. They strolled around the garden hand in hand . . . and of course I made clear that it was time they strolled to pastures new.

My next apology for a gardening assistant came in the shape of a teenage lad with earphones and a stereo radio tucked under his arm. I must say that he was a big help for the first hour or so, until I noticed that every time he smoked a strange-looking cigarette, the lawn-mower he was pushing started going round in circles, and I distinctly heard him yell, 'Spaced out, man . . . way out.' I wasn't sure what his new-found elation meant, until he climbed on top of the fence and stated that he was, and I quote, 'Flyin' high, baby . . .' He then flapped his arms, leapt off the fence and plummeted into the fish-pond. I began to feel that perhaps the strange-looking cigarettes were not wholly consistent with the policies laid down by tobacco companies, and so he had to go before he became 'spaced out' enough to imagine he was a Condor.

They came thick and fast after that: little men who said to me, 'Leave everything in our hands, sir,' then shot off to the pub with half my gardening tools and never came back, and a brooding old chap who spent the day under a weeping ash clutching his heart and eating things from a parcel.

Finally, my next-door neighbour sent his gardener round with the offer of 'Doing' four hours a day for me. He was a gardener, by Jupiter . . . He was quite elderly and gnarled, with eyes that were flecked with green. His knowledge of plant life was incredible and he was a workhorse. Within a month, he'd got the half acre looking quite magnificent and he taught me a

lot; he was very expensive but I would gladly have sold the family to keep him on. The only thing lacking between us as we toiled together was communication in speech. The problem was his dentures, which were so old they were made of ivory and they didn't fit. Thus one enjoyed this exchange:

Me: 'Good morning, George.'
Him: 'Gooshmashin.'
Me: 'I see you've stocked up the rockery.'
Him: 'Niiddeed yit lessme shell yu, mindeyu hit will coshed yulota smoni, butter use gosht to ghet thebeesst.'

When he first heard old George speak, the vicar asked me if

he was a Christian, and the village postmistress was convinced he was a Polish war criminal. But when George retired to live with his sister in Dorset, he was sadly missed, and when he shook my hand before leaving, he said quietly, 'Hallserbeeest, Mishter Dawrshun, Ivyenjooyed wurckink wishyu' . . . and I'll never forget those words.

With old George gone, I hadn't the inclination to seek another gardener so I carried on alone, and the task began to prove too much. Apart from the dreadful expense incurred, my stamina and enthusiasm took a bashing from the constant colds I endured and the aches and pains. By now, the wife had taken to overseeing the work and bringing food out to me on a plastic tray. If I paused for breath, she would shrill from the bedroom window and threaten me with a visit from her mother . . . That was the stimulus I needed to pick up the spade again.

Something had to be done and soon, that was frighteningly obvious – but what? There is no easy answer to this gardening business; a garden will cost you the earth, if you'll pardon the pun, and that is that. You might find the odd nursery that's cheaper than the others, but the expense is still hefty. In the world of garden maintenance, there are more cowboys than in Texas, and they can do more harm than good. With a small garden, you could, I suppose, have it cemented over, but Dame Nature will be annoyed and ere long, slender shoots will force their way through. Soon the area will look like a disused airfield, and cats will pee all over it. So what is the solution? Huddled under that tree, it came to me in a flash of inspiration: you have to get somebody else to take it on. But who?

The Dawson Humility Method

Buy two identical plants. Insert one in the soil, and hide the other one. Show the wife the plant that you've just bunged in the soil and say that it's a very difficult one to nurture, adding that it can take a certain talent to do so. She will of course sniff and tell you that it has no chance in your hands and stalk away muttering, 'Mother was right about him.'

At dawn the following day, creep into the garden after giving the wife a Mickey Finn, and damage the plant. On some pretext, get the wife outside and show her the injured plant, and don't forget to shake your head.

Repeat this practice for three days until the plant is totally knackered. Allow the wife to give you hell over the state of it, then sink to your knees and implore her to do something with it . . . Ten to one she will. Again at dawn the following day, tiptoe into the garden and fetch the other plant that you've hidden, uproot the battered one, and insert the healthy plant. Go indoors, take the wife a cup of tea and as she sips, simply stand with your cap in your hand and bow your head in humility. She'll glare at you, suspecting that you've lost money on a horse, then ask what the bloody hell's the matter.

Now is the time for drama. Raise your head and say breathlessly, 'Darling . . . What can I say, my turtle dove? Mine own precious angel . . . Please come into the garden.' About turn, and march out briskly as if covering a deep emotion. She'll follow you all right, if only to find out if you've been drinking. Point to the plant and say in ringing tones, 'HOW DID YOU DO IT?' She'll stoop and look at the thing in awe, and for once she'll be speechless.

I guarantee that from that moment on, she will be convinced

that she is the Messiah of the watering can. From that day forward, she will take over the care of the plants and the shrubs and the bushes; all you have to do then is make a cobblers of the lawn and she'll wrench the mower from your hands and do it herself.

You'll have all the time in the world to restore yourself to full health and rejoin the lads in the pub, while she flits about the half acre with a superior grin on her face. If you have an awkward wife who isn't bothered about the state of the garden, divorce her and grab a woman that is . . . Or you could try hypnotism, I suppose. I know a certain Dr Hans Schemmingfester . . .

Gardening Books

Popplewaite's Guide to Banana Tree Pruning in Oxford. (Monkeyshine Books, £45.95)

How to Grow a Dwarf Redwood in Tarmac – by Commersal Bindweede. (Certified Press, £1.99)

How to Smother Greenfly with a Blanket – by Miss Patricia Gumboil. (Hunter and Barber Ltd, £102.00)

How to Avoid Shopping

This is one of the most ghastly penalties of married life, and one that can send a man to bed drooling for his mother. There is little one can do about it; women are lost without an armful of parcels and don't feel fulfilled until their purses are mere vacuums.

You don't need me to conjure up the horrors of a High Street sale, do you? Where I live, they recently held a sale in a normally delightful emporium that caters to our whims in a somewhat dreamy fashion. A new owner decided that he would 'ginger things up' by holding the first reduction of prices ever seen in the above-mentioned establishment ... That decision changed the personalities of my neighbours for all time.

As the village clock boomed out 9 a.m., a tide of colourful humanity surged down the main street near our ignoble pile; it was like the opening shot of *Exodus* as the mighty living river flowed towards the hapless emporium. The din was unnerving and the faces of some of the notable village ladies were twisting into grimaces of hate as they trampled the weaker ones under the thundering high heels of the maddened herd. Old Miss Grimes, a gentle soul under normal circumstances and given to visiting the sick and needy, could now be seen sticking her giant hat-pin into the formidable buttocks of those who tried to overtake her in the race for a bargain. Dear Mrs Pillingwell, the sweet pillar of church hall fund-raising events, the saintly organiser of World War Two scrap metal drives, was now to be observed kicking shins in a frenzy as she ploughed a furrow into the emporium proper.

Knickers, frocks, garters, bolts of cloth, packets of tights, blouses, scarves, top coats, slips, bras and corsets were tugged to and fro as the battle raged through the store. Casualties mounted as the struggle for electric kettles, pots and pans, overblankets, underblankets, blankets with patterns on, blankets with none, perfumes, table centrepieces, glassware, glazed ducks and ceramic frogs changed hands in the heat of

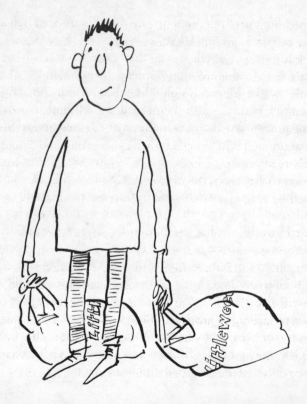

combat. The white-faced management of the store cowered as the village ladies tore one another to shreds.

Finally, the triumphant survivors of the holocaust poured forth from the ruined emporium waving their spoils aloft like banners or Sioux lodge standards. Many a tale of valour would be told during coffee mornings and many a wound would be licked before the dust of the sale settled. Of course the women loved it all. A mere male would have come out with his hands up; not so the 'weaker sex', already quietly planning strategies for the next bargain hunt.

Expeditions to shopping centres are something that a man will have to face up to if he decides to take unto himself a wife; the trick is to learn to avoid them.

It's useless mumbling about 'having something to do at home' on Saturday mornings – it's your job to drive her into town, park the car and then act as a pack-mule for the loot she'll grab. There is an alternative, of course: you can drop her off at the shopping precinct, then drive round and round until she's ready to be picked up, leap from the car and load the saloon with bundles before the traffic warden cops you . . . Not much of a choice, is it? Let's examine the pitfalls of both schemes.

First, there is the age old problem of parking the car. This knotty thorn will never go away so let's face the dilemma together. Our nation has a love affair with double yellow lines. They are everywhere in abundance and always situated where you need to park. Bribing a traffic warden isn't easy. To start with, the average warden has the intellect of a retarded pit pony and it would take a week for him to understand what you're offering the money for. If the warden is slightly effeminate, the money offer could be grossly misconstrued.

You could, of course, set the alarm clock for 3 a.m., have a hasty breakfast, then motor into town with a Thermos flask and park the damned car outside the store she wishes to plunder. If you have the same luck I have, you'll fall asleep until ten o'clock and wake to find the car surrounded by the FBI, the CID, a detachment of Gurkhas, and an official from the Bomb Squad. You'll be interrogated by a man with a limp and an Eton accent, and you will still get a ticket.

If, on the other hand, you decide to run your better half to the shopping parade and go round the block until she's finished (or in her words, 'I'll only be ten minutes, love'), beware. If there's one thing you need to remember, it is that women don't recall their vows when faced with a counter full of goodies. Off you'll weave through the pedestrians and the traffic as you commence the first circuit. It's fun for the first three runs but it begins to pall when your rambling circulation draws the attention of a rather vigilant policeman. Round and round you go, creating an exhaust fog and talking to yourself loudly. This will get you noticed by a startled motorist who knows a giant lorry-driver with a CB radio. The vigilant policeman has by now jotted down the number of your vehicle and the giant lorry-driver thinks you're a nut. She's been gone for over an hour and you've started to sob openly. Next you will probably run out of petrol in the main stream of traffic and the policeman will book you for intent to solicit in the High Street.

If the policeman's voice is heard too clearly, you may have to be rescued from a hostile crowd of neo-Baptists or thumped by the giant lorry-driver. Eventually your better half will emerge from the Stygian caves of merchandising and play merry hell with you for not being there on the spot to meet her.

Either way you cannot win or even score a draw, my friend, so you have to devise a plot to escape this awesome trap . . .

We are indebted to Gustave Cockle for this method of avoiding shopping and speaking as one who has carried out his plan to the letter, I can tell you that it jolly well works.

Gustave Cockle was born at an early age which meant that he fitted his pyjamas quite well. His father worked in a timber yard until he fell asleep on a plank in the rain and warped to death. His mother went round the country towing caravans for a living and did very well at it until her teeth dropped out. Alone and frightened, little Gustave was adopted by a Jewish kamikaze pilot who used to crash planes in his brother's scrap yard. That was such an old joke, Gustave left their house in disgust and went to live with his Aunt Jessie who had five daughters and only one bathroom. Gustave spent three years with his legs crossed before he could get in the bathroom for a pee and so he grew up with a hatred of women. His wonderful autobiography *Bladders were Meant to be Swollen* is a lesson to us all.

Avoid Shopping the Cockle Way

First, from Monday morning to Friday evening, say to the wife over and over again, 'We MUST go into town to shop on Saturday.' Mention casually that there is a certain store you have to visit, one you know she favours, and wax on about how divine it is. By Wednesday, if you keep at it, she will be firmly convinced that you've got a bit of stuff working there, so nudge this idea along by drenching yourself in an expensive after-shave and wearing a clean vest. An early photograph of Vesta Tilley might give her the hump but it would plant the physical idea of a rival for her man. When Friday night arrives, she will be steaming like an experimental kettle, and she may well dope your cocoa before you turn in. Imagine the luxury of sleeping throughout Saturday morning, rising just in time for the betting shop and the last races from Kempton. . . . Having doped you, the wife will then catch the bus to town and because she has no idiot chauffeur to bring her home, she'll spend less to ease her burden . . . first blood to you.

As the wife is increasingly shaken by the belief that you have a fancy piece in the potted meats section, you now have the chance to act out talking in your sleep . . . For example:

Wife: 'Harry?' (Shakes his shoulder.)

Husband: 'It's no use, I tell you . . . it can't be love . . . just lust.'

Wife: 'Wake up, Harry . . . you're dreaming again. Who are you talking about? Me?'

Husband: 'Must see you every Saturday . . . Got to, darling . . . my friend.'

Wife (belting husband with bolster): 'You bastard, who is she?'

Husband: 'I need your love and friendship . . . Since my marriage I seem to have lost touch with my old mates . . . Ah, the loneliness!'

Wife: 'I'll put a stop to your gallop, you randy sod. No more Saturday trips to town for you, lad.'

Pretend to wake up at the twentieth blow with the bolster and rub your eyes in a childlike manner.

Husband: 'Wha–What are you striking me for, beloved?'

Wife: 'You poxy little xxxxxx! Lying *?@£&$! Bloooooooody ——'

Husband: 'You are beside yourself, petal.'

Wife: 'I'll find out who she is, you swine – mark my words.'

Husband (stagger from bed to window – don't scratch, it spoils the effect): 'There could never be anybody else for me but you, my turtle dove. But sometimes I yearn for a friendship I knew in yesteryear . . .'

This is a tricky bit and no mistake. You are about to tell her how much you miss your mates at the club but she might misunderstand if you don't put it across correctly. She could think the 'friendship' is a cover-up for a mass leg-over in Safeways.

Wife: 'What the hell do you mean, "friendship"?'

Husband: 'I know you don't think much of Fred and Harry, my sweet, but I miss our chats on Saturdays down at the gardening centre. So when I meet someone who enjoys talking about plants and gardening generally . . .'

Wife: 'Plants, gardening? Since when have you taken any interest in the bloody garden, hey? It's me who damn well does it . . .'

Husband: 'I know it's you who does it, my little divinity, and that's why I've been reading and talking to people about horticulture so that I can share the peace and tranquillity of green-fingered gossip once more.'

Wife: 'Bullshit. Right, lad, you can see your stupid friends on Saturday mornings after you've driven me into town. But you had better pick me up at four o'clock in the afternoon, and don't smell of drink either.'

You haven't scored a total victory but it's not too bad. Once you've dropped her off in town, you can scoot back to the gardening centre, creep through the section where the bags of fertiliser are stacked, turn left past the garden furniture, open the exit door that is half concealed by a horde of Do-It-Yourself implements, stroll into a narrow alleyway, walk briskly down the main street and be in the club in time for the pulling of the first pint.

Should you become pissed, it is essential that your pals rally round. Hot black coffee must be administered, and something to take away the smell of alcohol from your breath. Finally, get one of the lads to follow a horse with a shovel, then smear your person with lumps of manure. You have now picked the wife up and she is holding her nose.

Wife: 'You stink, what the hell have you been doing, rolling in the sh—'

Husband: 'Sorry, love, but we've been down at an allotment. Harry and I are going to grow our own produce, organically as well.'

Wife: 'In that case don't bother picking me up at all, send a taxi instead.'

Isn't it worth it? For remember, while you spend on the cab at least you are saving on the black coffee and sundries, not forgetting the wear and tear on your nerves. The wife thinks she has scotched your little romance by allowing you access to your mates again, and all you have to do when rat-arsed with drink is to sprawl on the settee with a smear of manure on your shirt – the wife will leave you alone to sober up in sheer contentment. Don't forget to take home fresh vegetables from time to time and it's not a bad thought to forge an award for yourself from a gardening organisation. Also it is essential that you still pretend to talk in your sleep, but this time mutter about how happy you are with the wife . . .

It stinks to high heaven, doesn't it? Be careful not to overdo it, otherwise the wife will get frisky and . . . oh, God forbid.

Mr —— from Mumps Bridge in Oldham writes:

Cockle's method certainly helped me. I used it to such good effect, the wife left me and I'm a total alcoholic.

When I can remember who I am, I'm a happy little soul and I've got all the manure I need.

Mr Brolly writes from a secret address:

My life was a mess because of shopping. I even developed a rash through going into Tesco's. My wife never allowed me to open my mouth and yawning was a problem. Thanks to Cockle, my wife reeks of manure and she's always pissed. This gives me more time for setting fire to churches

Gustave Cockle was buried last spring; they had to bury him, he was dead. On his tombstone is etched a simple elegy:

He was, now isn't is he?

How to Rid Oneself of the Car Parking Stress Factor

We've touched briefly on the hazards of motoring and its effect on the human condition, and there is no longer any doubt about it: trying to find somewhere to park the car can shorten your life expectancy just as effectively as a hand grenade. Once you buy a motor vehicle, your blood pressure will never be the same again and in everybody's eyes you are a potential thug. The police lie in wait for you, traffic wardens stuff summonses into your hat-band, and pedestrians would cheerfully see you hunted down by renegade SAS.

Although we are told repeatedly that we live in an age of technological bliss, society has not yet come to terms with the motor car. Therefore the long arm of the law is pointed directly at you, the motorist.

Regarding the peril to your health in this matter, let us take my case as an example of how to age in one afternoon . . .

It was, I recall, a balmy day and the birds in the garden were busy doing their territorial tweets. My fairly new car shimmered on the driveway like a large puma and all augured well for a majestic jaunt to see an old friend who owned a pub on the coast. Trouble started almost immediately. As I backed out of the drive, I nearly ran down the vicar's wife who, once she'd recovered her composure, came out with a string of abuse that would have made the average stevedore sound like something out of *Playschool*. The tirade was followed by a left hook to the head as I wound the window down to apologise to the good lady.

With feathers somewhat ruffled, I weaved into the traffic stream and settled back to enjoy the ride. Within minutes my nerves were as tight as a hillbilly's banjo. Lorries sped past me and the rush of air sucked me into their polluted embrace; maniac drivers with glazed eyeballs hooted at me to move over as they crouched at their steering wheels as if in the Le Mans; and a police car pulled me over to the kerb.

Two giant law enforcers strode purposefully towards my panting vehicle and one of them sniffed my breath and said in a menacing tone, 'Good morning, Wing Commander.'

I tittered nervously and replied, 'Ha ha ha, Wing Commander . . . I'm not a wing commander.'

He looked puzzled. 'No, sir? Well, the speed you were doing made us assume you were low flying.'

'Speeding? Surely not, officer,' I croaked, 'I swear I wasn't doing more than thirty miles an hour.'

He smiled benignly and the other copper shook his head in rare disbelief.

'We clocked you at forty-seven miles per hour in a thirty mile limit,' my uniformed tormentor barked sternly. 'People like you are a menace on the roads.'

That did it. I rose stiffly to my full height outside the car and launched into a blistering diatribe about other drivers, and the articulated juggernauts which move my bowels in fear. I railed on about the law, democracy, corruption in high places and the cost of tinned soups . . . I cursed, begged, pleaded, sobbed . . . I was booked.

The central lane of the motorway was festooned with red cones and one needed six GCSEs to find a way out to the diversion. I lost count of the number of fists that were shaken at me by crimson-faced council workers leaning on their shovels. At my lowest ebb, I pulled into a service station for a dish of tea – and let's face it, you have to be at a low ebb to pay the prices those catering pirates demand. A gum-chewing lady with a cardboard hat on served me with a bacon sandwich and a weak pot of tea, and charged me a king's ransom for the ensuing indigestion.

Back on the motorway amid interchange madness, I decided to leave the roaring carnage and try a quiet country lane for the remainder of the trek. It was a mistake. A rumbling cart full of mixed manures stayed in front of me and the smell was positively mauve – twice I felt myself on the verge of passing out. Why we wax enthusiastic about rural life I will never know. It isn't just the odour, the inhabitants all stare at you as if you've just broken wind in a bucket, and most of them appear to have been recent guests in Rampton.

Eventually I arrived at the small resort in which my old friend carries on the noble art of innkeeping. The day just happened to coincide with a local pageant, didn't it. I drove round and round in an effort to park the damned car and there wasn't even space for a tricycle. I was beaten to the punch when a space did become available, and I decided to bribe a traffic warden. Such is the good fortune that constantly attends me, I had to choose the only incorrupt warden this side of Chicago, and off I trundled yet again. Finally, I found a spot in a field behind a high wooden fence and I silently thanked God for it . . . too soon, for a strangely familiar cart jerked to a halt on the other side and a mountain of mixed manures cascaded over my car in a hot pungent heap.

Overpowered by the stench, I crawled out of the débris but obviously could not avoid contact with the waste product. I stank to high heaven. When I reached the public house wherein my old friend held sway, half the customers fled and my pal wouldn't serve me.

Alone, soiled and depressed, I drove back home with the car windows lowered and contracted influenza. My wife threw away my clothing and my son in a fit of rare good humour suggested that I be rolled across the rhubarb patch to ensure a better crop.

That is why I became obsessed with finding some method of coping with parking the car, and it was while perusing a thirteenth-century book on Lincolnshire witchcraft that the germ of an idea came to me: a doppel-gänger. A doppel-gänger, as you well know, is a German word for a twin or a person who is your double, existing at the same time as you. I began haunting mortuaries to find a corpse that looked like me; unfortunately, with my complexion, I looked like all the other corpses, so I had to abandon the idea – so much for Lincolnshire witchcraft. There had to be a simpler notion, and eventually I found it.

The Dawson Car Parking Method

The first thing you need is a pair of legs, dummy legs that is, encased in ordinary trousers with the feet in socks and shoes. Get it? When you park the car on a double yellow line, ease the dummy legs halfway under the car engine so that it looks as if someone is repairing the thing, then open the bonnet lid or whatever you call it and Bingo! off you waltz to your assignment, knowing that your car will be left alone because people will think it's broken down.

Supposing a curious traffic warden decides to speak to the dummy legs? Well, all that is required is a tape recording of your voice uttering suitably mechanical phrases, for instance, 'Won't be a jiff . . . axle bearing's gone.' It's always wise to throw in a reference to the weather; after all, we are British are we not? If you have a few bob behind you, to allay further suspicion, a remote control unit can be operated which jerks the legs of the dummy as the tape recording is going on. This of course gives great authenticity and keeps dogs from peeing down the dummy's legs.

Don't worry about the traffic warden asking the tape recording questions – without the aid of an idiot board he won't be able to. But don't outstay your welcome; this trick will last only for about half an hour before the bobbies roll along with notebooks and pencils. If you wish to spend a longer period double-parked, then you must use the Dawson Inflatable Traffic Warden Kit. This full size replica with its own air cylinder can be inflated in seconds, and comes complete with spectacles and a vacant expression. Simply stand the warden kit by the driver's door and scoot off.

At a modest cost, you too can acquire this system which I say in all humility, is almost foolproof. I say 'almost' because if some bloody fool comes along with a pin and punctures the kit, the game's up and you'll be frogmarched off to some awful office painted green.

Of all the ills to beset mankind, the Video Menace must surely rank alongside the Plague, War, Famine and Drought as an evil to be bested.

It was my son who first introduced me to this awful piece of technology and turned me overnight into a myopic zombie. I recall bitterly that it was a cold dreary night, in fact so cold outside that brass monkeys were advertising for welders. Glancing through the newspaper, it became obvious that the television planners had quite forgotten the viewers as the evening's entertainment consisted of a rather bilious hour with Robin Day, an Australian soap opera that had about as much appeal as a lecture on the mating habits of a Malay dung-beetle, and a black and white film that was so old, the Red Indians attacking the fort meant it . . . and Gabby Hayes got the girl.

Moodily, I suggested to the family that we had a game of 'Monopoly' but half the bits were missing and Grandma cheats anyway, so it looked very much as if the night was well and truly knackered. At that moment, my son leapt to his sneakers and did a sort of 7th Cavalry, vanishing into the village and returning later with two video films rented for the sum of two pounds fifty pence per copy. Great, thought I, and settled down with a mug of scalding tea to watch avidly as my offspring bunged the film into the video player that had lain dormant under the Ferguson 26-inch set for months. (I'd never used it – I couldn't get the hang of pre-recording things.)

The video flickered into animation, bringing first a dire warning not to reproduce the film otherwise somebody awful would take me away in restraint, then snippets of future delights and finally the main feature: *It Came from Underneath the Sea*.

This was an incredible exercise in hokum, but immensely enjoyable. Briefly, the plot consisted of an underwater volcano blowing up the seabed and exposing a nest of three-legged haddocks with meat-eating tendencies who promptly swallowed a submarine and half the US Airforce. Before they were atom bombed, one of the monster haddock raped a lady scientist and she gave birth to a nineteen-pound deformed whitebait which grew very quickly and ate New Jersey. From that night on, I was hooked on videos.

I took to creeping into shops that rented these abominations and I never left without at least three of the damned things under my cardigan. Night after night I sat glued to such epics as *Nightmare on Elm Street*, *The Exorcist*, *Blood of the Vampire* and *The Beast in the Cellar*. Before long I was a member of at least four video rental establishments and the cost of hiring grew to epidemic proportions. I was faced with penury. I went to see our local doctor about my affliction but it turned out he was a bigger addict than me and we finished up watching six pre-recorded episodes of *Dr Kildare*.

Acting on a tip from my good friend Dr Schemmingfester, I managed to kick the habit of horror videos by looking at a copy of my mortgage every day, and there is no bigger horror than that.

Then, alas, I was introduced to a new and awesome attraction from the twilight world of the video: the Blockbuster. Huge sweeping mammoth films lasting up to eight hours . . . oh joy of joys.

By this time, my family had abandoned me and I didn't even know they'd gone. Two of my children had joined the Spanish Foreign Legion and my eldest girl had entered a convent. I cared not a jot; my world was a shimmering series of blockbusters and mini blockbusters; my world was full of music, laughter and tears from a reel of film, and the house stank.

My neighbours started avoiding my shambling ill-kempt figure and dogs barked at me. While waiting for a blockbuster that I'd ordered to arrive, I would roam around waste ground with other video addicts now reduced to derelicts by their habit. We'd huddle together in heaps of rubble and talk about the desire for another look at *An Affair to Remember* or a re-run of *The Thorn Birds*. They were my buddies and when I cried, they cried with me. Boy, did I go downhill fast. Soon

I was evicted for not paying the mortgage, and the police stopped me from trying to plug my video recorder into streetlamps. I fought with them, I spat abuse at them, and finally they dragged me off to prison. I stood in the dock with other examples of human flotsam and heard the words of condemnation hurled at me by my peers. I had sunk to the very bottom of the pile (and let's face it, that's where you'll find a pile – at the bottom).

An understanding magistrate refused to send me to jail. Instead she ordered me to attend Dr Potter's clinic for video addicts. My heart lifted at the knowledge that I had been given another chance and I couldn't wait to begin treatment at the clinic, which was situated in a charming mountain village in Cambodia. When the good Dr Potter knew that I had struck up a friendship with Schemmingfester, he took me under his wing as it were and helped me through the drying out process.

Oh those dreadful first few weeks! In place of a full video recording, the male nurses would allow us inmates only ten minutes of cartoons; when we craved for more Bugs Bunny we were knocked senseless to the ground by the caring staff. My nights were spent shackled by chains to the bed as I tossed and sweated in the ordeal of withdrawal. Spittle oozed down the side of my swollen lips as I pleaded for a copy of *Ghostbusters* or even *Rambo . . . First Blood*. At times I knew that I was losing my mind and it was Dr Potter who cradled my head during those long terrible nights, saving my beleaguered sanity.

Slowly my health returned, so that I could switch off *Neighbours* without feeling depressed – although there were times when the need for *Sesame Street* would send me scuttling for a sedative. Yes, there was light at the end of the tunnel and I vowed that if I ever achieved a full recovery, I would help other sufferers to overcome their addiction.

Today, a year after I left Potter's clinic, I still have to face up to the fact that I could go back into a world of utter degradation, and I take one day at a time. Last night I held an informal meeting for people who are suffering the horrors of video addiction, and we held hands and sang jingles from TV commercials to strengthen our resolve not to hire out *Rocky 3*.

There are many theories as to how one should tackle the problem of video addiction, and most of them are ridiculous. Some odd characters suggest that one should look at a film video backwards through a mirror, though this can also be habit-forming: one wretched chap I knew took to living that way and started walking out backwards to make it look as if he was coming in. His wife got fed up with him talking back to front and went home to her mother; he ran after her backwards and got run over by a tractor which was fortunately going in reverse at the time so he died happy, if you see what I'm driving at.

Another method is to turn the sound off and look at the screen upside down, by standing on your head or bending over and peering between your legs. There is danger in this idea – blood can rush to the head and cause cerebral palsy, or if you bend down at an inopportune moment, a sex-maddened Angus bull might wander past . . .

There is only one sure way to prevent video addiction and I know it works. First, stand about two feet from the television set having initially loaded the recorder with a film. Take several deep breaths until a yoga-type serenity is reached, and I am not against the use of rosary beads at this stage, or the massaging of a goat's horn if one is a Druid. Now, stretch to full height, expand the chest cavity, close the eyes firmly, draw back the right foot and kick the bloody television set in.

... and so it was that the leading citizen of the town was honoured on *This is Your Life*. The Master of Ceremonies said to him, 'Yours is a story that will give the youth of this nation the drive to go forth and succeed. You came to this town a young man; all you owned was a pair of trousers and a sweater, and all you carried was a stick over your shoulder with a cloth bundle on the end of it . . . yet within six months, you owned the largest hotel and theatre, three restaurants and two banks. It is a story that is legend in the world of commerce and high finance. The country waits for you to tell us one thing: what was in that cloth bundle?'

The man blew a wreath of cigar smoke into the camera lens and said, 'Forty million pounds.'

Let's not kid ourselves, work is bad for you: too much stress in looking for the best job available, and too much stress in keeping it if you find it. You leave school with a light shining in your eyes as you set out to get to the top of the heap, and years later, through poor diet, lack of exercise and too much responsibility, there's another light shining in your eyes as the doctor examines you after the coronary.

You have spent years being nice to the right people and worked long hours with only time to snatch the odd sandwich in between buttering up those you imagined would advance your career. Of course it has paid off in some ways. Your house is the biggest in the best part of town and you are proud of it. It's so big the mice wear St Christopher medals, and when it's three o'clock in the kitchen, it's half seven in the lounge. But you only see the blessed mansion in the morning and late in the evening. You have a full time landscape gardener who is robbing you blind, and a swimming pool that is maintained by a lusty youth who's giving your eldest daughter one and charging you a fortune for chlorine.

Your wife is involved with coffee mornings, relief for the Sudan, whist drives, hair appointments and dress fittings and she's on a slimming kick that's drained all the flesh away so that now, when she bends down, she looks like a question mark. She's too tired for sex and you've got yourself into a situation with a girl from the typing pool who's late with her monthlies, and has tapes of everything you've ever panted in bed.

You are Mr Success: the bank balance is robust, you are invited to all the functions, the Porsche snuggles alongside the Land Rover and E-type, the new nanny for the kids is a cert – so why don't you sleep at nights?

The reason is obvious. You've got it all, friend, but for how long? Your age is thirty-seven, but in big business you are an old man. Sure, you play squash and jog a little, but eyes are watching for one mistake and then . . . Bingo! it's a sideways promotion until decay sets in. The pundits thunder, 'Hard work never killed anybody.' Big deal, but what does it bring? A lousy watch and a pension. Where did the years go? The kids have grown up and buggered off, the house is too big and the wife is President of the local Darby and Joan club. Nobody remembers you and the fellow you played golf with dropped dead on the ninth green.

Age creeps on and you and the wife are so deaf, you've started having to shout sweet nothings to each other. One of the grandchildren asks you to do an impression of a frog and when you ask him why, the tot replies, ' 'Cos Daddy said we'll have a lot of money when Grandad croaks.'

Isn't it bloody awful? It doesn't matter what your station in life may be, you cannot win. It's no good 'dropping out' either. What's the point in chanting 'Hare Krishna' under a viaduct with bald-headed gurus and a reformed call girl with rabies?

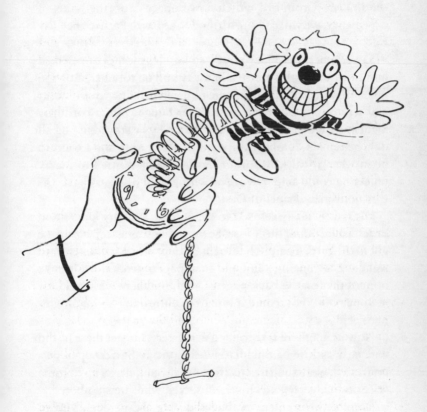

Being a criminal isn't the answer. It's still hard work breaking into places and the threat of jail and incarceration with a known sex offender might lead to a change in your outlook and a sore bottom.

133

So what is the solution? You want security and money and an easy, stress-free life, but how?

Allow me to point the way through the method employed by a certain Mr Cromford Ffitch-Sawcropper. For the sake of expediency, we will call the method 'The Ffitch Path to the Easy Life'.

Sawcropper was a lazy youth, so lazy his mother once asked him to let the bathwater drain away and he told her, 'It's too much trouble.' He spent so much time in bed that to save wear and tear on his pyjamas, his mother bought him a corduroy nightshirt. When someone asked him why he stayed in bed all day, he replied, 'Opportunity only knocks once and I want to be in when it calls.' Rumour has it that he refused to marry unless he could find a woman who would agree to have the ceremony in a Chapel of Rest.

His father finally refused to support his son any longer and ordered him out of the house. Sawcropper was asleep before he got to the garden gate. That night he slept on a park bench, and as he was arranging some old newspapers around his legs he noticed that on the back page of a tabloid there was an ad for volunteers at a government research centre that was investigating sleep.

How he got there is shrouded in mystery, but get there he did and he was hired immediately. Every day Sawcropper was undressed, put to bed in a mirrored bedroom, wired up to some scientific gadgetry and closely observed while he slumbered.

Despite Government cutbacks during the perennial economic depression, Sawcropper was kept on at the centre – mainly because frustrated nursing sisters used his body for relief while he was asleep. He is still there now. Scientists are using him to explore the possibility of cybernetic sleep for astronauts who fancy a trip to Pluto. He eats three meals a day, he's paid a wage which goes straight into his Swiss bank account, and he's getting more than enough sex (although he doesn't know it).

The Ffitch Path is an excellent ploy to avoid work and I strongly advocate that you try it. For those of you who are interested, I heartily recommend you contact a certain Dr Hans Schemmingfester though at present he is in East Borneo leading a team of boffins studying the reasons why a Malay dung-beetle gets an erection when they take its gall bladder out in a pan of soap.

You can get in touch with the good doctor at this address:

> Minsky's Bar
> Futtle Strasse
> Cologne

There are various sleep centres up and down the country, perhaps the most famous being the House of Lords.

If you have a problem sleeping, don't be put off trying this method. For a small fee, a chemist I know in Bayswater will hand you a phial of chloroform for use on entry to a centre and some smelling salts to rouse you in case a nurse gets randy.

Many men have tried this system on my recommendation and so far I have had no complaints whatsoever. Occasionally, the odd feminist gets worked up about it being a male preserve but that can be handled by casually mentioning that your bowels have to be moved for you, and you have no clean underwear if you have an accident.

Let us now study another method of avoiding work. This one we will entitle 'The Godfrey Radishfogg Way'. Radishfogg was so lazy, his mother had to lie at his side in bed and breathe for him. Nevertheless he came up with an idea for getting paid for nothing which, in its own small way, is a gem.

He walked into a bank one morning and said to the manager, 'Please don't send me any more letters asking me if I want to borrow money from you.' Before the startled manager had a chance to reply, Radishfogg walked out briskly and entered another bank, a rival branch of the one he'd just been in. This time he strode up to the manager and said, 'If you want to handle my account, you will have to prove that you carry sufficient funds, should I need to withdraw the odd half million or so. I'm sure my other bank across the road will vouch for my integrity.' Again, before the manager could answer, Radish-fogg trotted out.

He then retraced his steps to the first bank, made as if to speak to the manager but seemed to think better of it and left. At lunchtime, both bank managers met as usual in the Swan and Trumpet, wary of each other as always. This conversation ensued:

2nd manager: 'Busy time, old boy?'
1st manager: 'Quite. Lot of currency movement about, I've noticed.'
2nd manager: 'Yes. Mind you, I had an idiot in earlier who wanted to know if we carried sufficient funds, in case he needed to withdraw the odd half million or so, ha ha ha.'
1st manager: 'Good grief, that's one for the book and no mistake. I had a lunatic in myself who insisted that I mustn't suggest a loan, ha ha ha.'
2nd manager (frowning in concentration): 'This crackpot, was he a tall dark-haired man? Slightly bald, on the thin side?'
1st manager: 'That's correct.'

Now both managers are thinking, 'Suppose this man isn't a

crackpot . . .' After all, he didn't want a loan, and a bank manager will only offer a loan to somebody providing he can prove he doesn't need it.

The managers will curtail their lunch break and scamper back to their respective offices, hell bent on trying to get information on Radishfogg. I should remark that at this stage Radishfogg spent some time poring over the financial columns of the country's leading newspapers until he came across a photograph of an industrial giant whom he resembled. The research paid off. Two days after his initial confrontation with the bank managers, Radishfogg saw the photograph of Kamel Fazlid, the richest Arab prince in Durham. All Radishfogg had to do now was strip his bed of a sheet and wear it. This he did and he re-entered the first bank stationing himself near the manager's office. A teller, curious about Radishfogg's attire, hurried in to tell his chief about the apparition outside. The manager rose and had a peep at Radishfogg, giggled nervously and was about to order the teller to call the police when he looked at Radishfogg again. He glanced down at his copy of the *Financial Times*, gulped heavily and his eyes lit up with avarice.

'Don't stand there gawping, ask the gentleman if I could have a word with him,' he said nastily, washing his hands the while.

With massive aplomb, Radishfogg billowed into the manager's office and stood proudly in his sheet before the cringing manager.

Yes, said Radishfogg, he had approached the manager two days ago asking him not to proffer a loan; yes, he had done it for a reason. 'My country is building a series of salmon farms in dried wadis near Iraq and because of the political turmoil there it could be disastrous if word leaked out that I was shipping huge funds to Britain. The reason I said, "Please don't send me any more letters asking me if I want to borrow money from you", was because a secret agent named Hashmil had been following me around the City and into your bank.'

The manager was stunned by all these revelations of international intrigue, and his senses swam. If he could foist a whopping great loan onto this Arab, the interest gleaned from it would secure his future for ever – why, it might even mean he could afford a Ford Sierra after all . . .

It took him the best part of two hours to talk Radishfogg into borrowing two hundred and fifty thousand pounds, the amount all in fifty pound notes. ('Has to be cash, effendi. That way the secret agent from Iraq won't smell a rat, or a salmon for that matter,' said Radishfogg sternly.)

Radishfogg left the first bank, walked across the road to the other one, told the manager he thought he was a good risk for his money and deposited his quarter of a million. Except for a few thousand in an ordinary deposit account, he put it all in a high yield one. The second manager was delighted to be of service to Kamel Fazlid, who for the sake of security would draw out his money under the name of Radishfogg. They both laughed dutifully at the silly name and shook hands.

Radishfogg left the manager of the second bank dreaming of promotion, a trip to Hollywood, a new car (possibly a Mercedes Benz – he already had a Ford Sierra) and taking on a mistress.

The interest on the high yield account would be used to pay off his loan to the first bank, and that way nobody could accuse him of fraud. As old Foggy spent most of his time in bed, his wants were few and the money would last him some time – thus was the desire for sloth sated on the greed of others. It's not a scheme I would personally endorse; it's not only full of perils, it's bloody stupid.

Incidentally, some easy money can be picked up by backing horses and I overheard two Japanese businessmen mention two horses that couldn't lose. One was called 荻ノカムイオー and the other one 光デュール

Have a bob or whatever on 'em.

Money Matters

Money worries top the bill when it comes to 'Things that are Bad for You' and I wish there was an easy method of ridding ourselves of this problem but there isn't, I'm afraid. However, mayhap we can find a way to make things a bit smoother.

Income tax is a terrible indictment of our age. There is a new tax form coming out shortly and there are only two questions on it: (a) how much did you earn last year? and (b) . . . send it. It is an absolute imposition in my view and gives me a headache that rages for days after I receive a demand. I've tried begging for mercy and a longer period to pay; I've tried blackmail after snapping a tax inspector in a hot embrace with a well-known strumpet in a Wimpy bar (that didn't work out because the cover hadn't been removed from the camera lens, and I fell off the ladder); I've borrowed children and dragged them in rags to our local office to plead for clemency and a rebate . . . Nothing.

There is only one way to beat the tax people . . . and that is, arson. To be perfectly frank, this method can cost a lot of money unless you know someone who sells petrol on the cheap. You need detailed plans of every tax office and the ability to hitchhike all over the country in order to save on train fares. It is necessary to wear a series of disguises: stage beards, moustaches, false noses and ears plus wigs of various lengths, and an inflatable hump is a huge asset. Next you must prepare an arsenal of petrol bombs or Molotov Cocktails – for technical advice, try your friendly neighbourhood anarchist.

Second-hand knapsack on your back and with a suitcase

crammed with inflammable materials, you are now set to commit arson on all the country's tax offices. If you play your cards right, you might get sponsorship from a disgruntled assassin or a group of Franco fans. To do any serious good, you have to keep on the move and get the flames really going before the fire brigade arrive.

For heaven's sake don't try to claim V A T back on the petrol, that's a sure way to be nabbed. If arrested and sent to prison you could be regarded as a martyr; who knows, on release with good behaviour you might get to stand as a Liberal in a by-election.

The housekeeping budget is another source of dissent that won't go away no matter how one ignores it. Women and money are twin elements; neither can exist without the other. However much you give women, they will always need more – this is a tricky area and no mistake.

Some years ago my own dear spouse roared in her dulcet tones that she couldn't manage the housekeeping on five pounds a week. I hesitated not a whit, straight away I doubled it . . . now she gets five pounds a fortnight. She became known in the family as the 'Lone Ranger' because she was always looking through my pockets for silver.

There is no effective method to stop women from demanding more housekeeping money: Schemmingfester recommends repeatedly selling one's house and buying a smaller one; thus, he argues, you can reduce the housekeeping budget as the house decreases in size. Between you and me, it's a daft notion to say the least, but I can't bring myself to tell him.

Tipping is another stress provoker in my view. I never seem to get it right; either I give too little which earns me a sneer, or I

Les Dawson Gives Up

give too much and that earns me a smirk and a whispered 'flash bastard'.

Why the hell should we tip people? A tip is nothing more than a bribe, is it not? I've known perfectly sane folk go to pieces in a restaurant when it came to tipping the waiter, and they've thrown up in a tureen. A nice chap of my acquaintance used to cry in taxis when it came to the end of the journey, and he's often been seen clutching a taxi driver's knees as he begged forgiveness for the minuscule tip. This quite ridiculous custom has often spoiled an evening on the town, especially at the Savoy where the maître d'hôtel makes you feel positively toadlike.

There is a good way out of this business. Simply buy some teabags, wrap each one separately in a medium-sized box, mark clearly in stencil 'Handle with Care' and then, after say a cab ride home, pay the man and as an afterthought hand him one of the packages, saying as you do so, 'God bless you and have a drink on me.' He will think you've given him a bottle of something rather precious and he won't dare open the box until he gets home in case he damages the contents in the taxi. By the time he finds the teabag, you'll be well away and he'll vent his spleen on the cat.

The trouble with this method is that you have to carry a lot of packaged teabags about with you – in this day and age you have to drop sums of money even to get a smile, let alone any service. The answer to this is to buy a sailor's kitbag from the Army and Navy Stores – they're quite cheap and hold a lot. Unfortunately this brings its own problems: suspicious constables will think you're a regular Bill Sykes, and at Christmas you could be mugged by toffee-ridden kids.

*

As a means to attain the easy life, many people turn to gambling. Don't. As a stress factor it is one of the worst possible things to indulge in. For years I enjoyed a flutter on the horses but I had no luck with them. I once backed a horse in the Grand National and it fell in the paddock.

I tried dog racing. Eagerly I invested money in a greyhound called Flash but that dog was so slow, the first time we ran it at White City the hare bit its leg. Disgruntled and depressed, my partner and I walked back to our cheap hotel near the Grand Union Canal with the infernal animal trotting breathlessly behind us.

'Let's get rid of it,' said my partner.

I nodded in agreement. 'We have no choice . . . What do you suggest?'

He replied sagely, 'Let's throw it in the canal.'

I shook my head. 'There's no need, let's just run away from it.'

The football pools are capable of bringing on a cardiac arrest. I have never gone in, as it were, for that type of gamble so I am incapable of understanding the fervour in someone's voice when they shout, 'My draws are up.' I would have thought that anybody with breeding would have made sure that their drawers were well up.

The only way you will win at gambling is to hold up a betting shop with a machine pistol or rush in and shout, 'Ladbroke's is on fire.'

Summing Up

... and so it was written in *The Lost Book of the Old Ones* that whoever should defile the tomb of the Sacred Ram would suffer the torment of dismemberment, and for centuries the tomb was left severely alone.

In the spring of '67, Miss Agnes Brimmington-Peach defied the ancient curse, broke into the tomb and ransacked the treasures within. Two hours later, after a take-away prawn curry and chips, she felt the need to visit the canvas latrine that sat near an outcrop in the desert. As she strained on the makeshift commode, reading a back copy of *Radio Times*, her left leg fell off ... the curse had struck. Six months later, back home in her native Yorkshire, she cried heavily on her mother's shoulder and lamented, 'Mummy, I am doomed to be a spinster for the rest of my life, no man will want to marry a woman with only one leg.'

'Fiddlesticks,' snorted her mother. 'One day, my girl, you'll leave this house and as you walk down the main street, you'll meet the man of your dreams, and he'll sweep you off your foot.'

(Well, it seemed funny at the time ...)

In essence, nothing we enjoy is good for us, is it? In times gone by, people got on with their lives and if some fool got stroppy, one gunboat up the Nile was enough to put the wind up their dhotis. Before the First World War, civilisation was groping towards enlightenment for all strata of society, but the war not only decimated the cream of European manhood, it destroyed the dignity of that age. In the Edwardian era, chorus girls could marry a duke; nowadays, despite female liberation, a girl is lucky to meet a lad who hasn't beaten up a pensioner. The Twenties gave us the Depression, Elliot Ness and the Charleston; but nothing intellectual either in politics or morality. The Thirties saw the advent of manufactured warfare in order to goad the world's economy back to life ... The Spanish Civil War became a testing ground for new weapons, new political doctrines, and a decent black shirt for Hitler.

Then came the Second World War and the Atomic Age, coupled with technical achievements that overshadowed humanity and its needs. Any old peasant could conceive a child but a fighter bomber cost money, and so life became cheap. The fact that the human body is the finest machine ever devised was overlooked in the frenetic neo-scientific technological world, and the race for material assets robbed us of the one thing that separates man from the animals ... compassion.

The church lost its meaning as it fought within its own power structure, and so must bear the responsibility for spiritual bigotry. Politics lost its purpose in the battle for power – and the promises made to a bewildered populace served to destroy any attempt to weld society into one unit. The family lost compassion in the scramble to out-do the Smiths next door, and instead of a child knowing the love of a full time mother and father, the playschool and nursery became parents as the mum and dad worked to accumulate objects.

So we're back to square one. Society is crippling us with the price we have to pay for the so-called Good Life, and the stress incurred in the race is too heavy a penalty. Of course the pundits won't admit that fact, will they? So fags, booze, a plate of chips and a well-groomed sausage are framed as the villains responsible for your early demise.

Doubtless by now you are spluttering the question, 'What

the hell can we do about it?' Good point. I've thought about it over and over again and I'm still buggered if I know.

In the struggle to find a stress-free life, I think it is wise to ponder on the sort of people you have around you. For instance, if your relatives are eager beaver types, always on the go, then get rid of them immediately. It is essential that, as a lazy sod, your circle of friends and loved ones should be of the same ilk.

I have always detested heroic people – they cause such a mess, don't they? I have always thanked the Almighty that my family were cowards of the first water. My great-great-grandfather fought with Wellington – they couldn't trust him with a gun. My great-grandfather tried to surrender so many times during the Boer War, he won the concession for the sale of white flags. They say his arms were in the air so often his elbows withered. Grandfather Dawson was on the Somme in the First World War when the first shot was fired; he was under a settee in Crewe when the second one went off. In one battle, while running away from the Germans, he was peppered with so many bullets in his rump, they didn't bury him, they weighed him in for scrap.

I am very proud of my father's war record, it's Flanagan and Allen singing 'Run Rabbit Run'. Dear Daddy had so many white feathers sent to him during the Second World War, he played the Oldham Empire for four years as Mother Goose. He was a wonderful man, was my dad – he was so yellow, he once cancelled a holiday in Jersey when he heard about the Battle of the Flowers. He was court-martialled for not getting out of bed in the mornings. The prosecuting officer said to him, 'Don't you ever hear the bugle call in the mornings?' Daddy replied, 'No sir, they always play it whilst I'm asleep.'

It is the hero image that creates war and stuff and the sooner we learn just to curl up somewhere and give in, the better off we'll be.

Frankly, the only sane way to survive, is to shack up with a deaf and dumb nymphomaniac who owns a pub. I'm not saying that it will necessarily lengthen your lifespan, but at least the only stress you'll have is keeping her happy and making sure you have a regular supply of ginseng and Boots rubbers.

The day is not far off, my fine feathered friends, when the powers that be will make it an offence to weigh more than seven stone three, and meat-eaters will be branded on the forehead with a tin of rancid Fray Bentos and sent to work in Vietnamese latrines. Cigarettes and alcohol will be totally banned and anyone found smuggling them into an office 'do' will be committed into the care of Lord Longford.

Having said that, I cannot see any gleam of light at present

but I must add that there is an underground movement taking shape in most major cities. In Manchester, for instance, in a disused whalebone trimmer's yard, fag smokers meet and puff away three times a week down a culvert. In Leeds, beer drinkers meet at the rear of a zoo and quaff secretly in the lion house. It's a risky business, and several rebels have been eaten after mistaking the lions for labradors. Fat people get together in North Acton, and if your trousers don't have a gusset down the back, you are regarded as a spy and force-fed on lumps of Cadbury's.

If you wish to fight the system and join the smouldering rebellion, hereunder are some useful contacts.

Leeds: Ferrington Bealkipper, alias 'The Shadow'. Celebrated alcoholic and amateur dentist. Lives under a wine store with his one-legged cousin who brews nettle beer. Distinguishing feature, a bright red nose and a tendency to sag to the left.

Manchester: 'Nicotine Al', sometimes known as Sarah on a bad day. Smokes over a hundred cigarettes a day and there's nothing wrong with his lung. Rolls dried tea-leaves for beginners and has trouble with his lower colon if he forgets to add milk and sugar. Used to expose himself in front of non-smokers in cinema queues and was arrested for throwing a bottle of Domestos over a vicar's hat. (He was convicted of a bleach of the priest.)

North Acton: George 'Tubby' Fauntlebaum. Champion pork scratchings hero and lapsed rabbi. Weighs in at twenty-four stone in his string vest and his ambition is to wipe his own bottom. Once bent down in front of his house and his neighbour thought he'd painted the garage. Supplies hamburgers to converted vegetarians outside a bookmaker's on Thursday afternoons from a pick-up van. Can be dangerous if he belches after onion rings.

If this book gets published I will, in all probability, be taken somewhere for treatment. However, I think I have indicated a few ways in which stress can be averted, and if I have done just that, then the exercise has been worthwhile.

The human spirit will always be a beacon in the fight against the dreadful encroachment of a too developed society that engulfs us with artifacts. We come into this world with nothing, and the VAT and income tax men will make damn sure we leave it with nothing. What is wealth? Can it buy the smile of a pretty girl? Of course it can.

In conclusion, I would like to thank several people for their help in collecting data for this book. To Jim (wanted in Harrow) . . . for his advice on how to shave the edges off a rabbit. To Davinia . . . for long nights in the bike shed and her help in plucking the eyebrows from an elderly trout wholesaler. And I mustn't forget Alf and Kevin who gave up watching their feet to assist me in looking for a box of marked dominoes in Selfridges.

Live your life to the full and always remember the old saying: 'A little of what you fancy does you good.' It's an old truism, especially if you're having it off with a midget. As old age approaches, don't be sad – think of what you have to look forward to: increasing deafness, poor circulation, failing eyesight, bladder trouble, ulcers and varicose veins . . . Why, you could become President of the United States.

Thanks to this immortal tome, the gateway to freedom is yours and that is all I could wish for ... Money? Riches? Never. If I have written this book purely for material gain, then may the Gods make sure that I never type another word, and that is something none of us wa

(oh shit)